THE BEST OF
Meister Eckhart

THE BEST OF
Meister Eckhart

EDITED BY HALCYON BACKHOUSE

Crossroad · New York

1996

The Crossroad Publishing Company
370 Lexington Avenue
New York, NY 10017

Copyright © Halcyon Backhouse 1992.

Printed in the United States of America

Library of Congress Cataloging-in-Publication Data

Eckhart, Meister, d. 1327
    [Selections. English. 1993]
The Best of Meister Eckhart / edited by Halcyon Backhouse.
        p.   cm.
    ISBN 0-8245-1262-6 (pbk.)
    1. Mysticism—Catholic Church—Miscellanea.   2. Catholic Church—
Sermons.   3. Sermons, English.   4. Catholic Church—Doctrines.
I. Backhouse, Halcyon C.   II. Title.
BV5080.E3213   1993
248.2'2—dc20   92–29381
                                                          CIP

CONTENTS

EDITOR'S INTRODUCTION

Franz Pfeiffer's scholarly edition of *Meister Eckhart*, published in Leipzig in 1857, remains the earliest and the largest collection of Eckhart's writings. It was translated into English by C. de B. Evans and published in London by John M. Watkins in 1924. This new edition is based on Evans' translation, and the following amended extract is taken from Evans' introduction to the 1924 edition:

Eckhart has been called the father of the German mystics and the philosophical creative genius of the German mystics. According to Dean Inge, Eckhart is 'next to Plotinus the greatest philosopher-mystic' and the most Plotinian of all Christian philosophers. He was a learned member of the Dominican or Preaching Order, and it was at the Dominican College of St Jacob that he was given the title *Meister* by Pope Boniface VIII.

But it was principally at Strasbourg and afterwards at Cologne that he established his great influence as a teacher and 'for an entire generation, with the boldest freedom, preached to the multitudes in the German tongue on topics bristling with difficulties for the orthodox faith'. For he had conceived the then novel idea of instructing the laity and the many semi-religious communities and brotherhoods of that date – Beguines, Beghards, Friends of God, etc. – no less than the religious of his Order, and for this purpose it was necessary to make the further innovation of using German instead of Latin, the teaching medium of that day.

Eckhart's success at expounding the abstruse tenets of the Scholastic philosophy in an undeveloped language which he had to supply with words and fashion to his needs, earned him the titles of father of the German language and father of German philosophic prose. The church authorities became alarmed at the enthusiasm roused by his teaching and especially at its effect on the laity. He was accused of preaching to the people in their own language things that might lead to heresy. This led to his excommunication in 1329, after his death, on the general grounds of preaching to the laity the secrets of the Church, a list of seventeen specific heretical and eleven objectionable doctrines being appended to the indictment.

To the first accusation Eckhart replied: 'If the ignorant are not taught they will never learn; the business of the doctor is to heal.' The charge of heresy he strenuously denied and largely succeeded in rebutting while he lived. 'I protest in the presence of God,' he said, 'that I have always avoided with horror all error in matters of faith.' Eckhart never made any recantation of his teaching, though he publicly declared his willingness to retract any error 'that might be proved against him'.

There is only the scantiest of material for a biography of Eckhart. We do not know where or when he was born. It is argued that he was born before 1260 either at Strasbourg in Saxony, or at Hochheim in Thüringia. The first known mention of his name is in a list of Professors at the University of Paris in

1302. In 1303 he was Provincial of the Order in Saxony, with its sixty convents, men's and women's. To this title he added in 1307 that of Vicar-General of Bohemia, where he reformed the religious houses. In 1311 he returned to Paris University and in 1312 began his long sojourn as head of the Order at Strasbourg. Eight years later (1320) he was Prior of Frankfurt. There was now some suspicion of his orthodoxy but the Order still supported him and he was given a Chair at the Dominican College in Cologne, where he enhanced his reputation as a preacher. Here Tauler, Suso and Ruysbroeck probably heard him. In 1325–26 suspicion of his teaching brought him before the Inquisition in Venice. He delivered his Protest before that body and then on 13 February 1327 made his public Declaration of orthodoxy in the Dominican Church at Cologne. That was the last date Eckhart was known to be alive.

The answer of the Inquisition to his appellation, refusing to accept it, is dated 22 February 1327, and it is conjectured that Eckhart died soon after. He was excommunicated by the Bull of John XXII, 27 March 1329.

After that Eckhart lost all but legendary fame and his writings survived mostly under other names. In 1829, five hundred years later, Gorres speaks of him as *une figure chrétienne presque mythique!* But for at least two generations after his death his writings, secretly passed from hand to hand and frequently transcribed, formed what Lasson calls 'the text-books of God-intoxicated piety'.

To the preachers of Eckhart's school, John Tauler, Suso, Ruysbroeck, all members of the Brotherhood of the Friends of God, and to others of less note, his writings were a veritable mine from which they drew not only inspiration but words, sayings, whole passages and even whole sermons.

Eckhart did not just write for theologians but also for ordinary men and women. This is why he wrote in German and not in Latin. It is hoped that this abridged edition will make available to a wide readership some of the sermons and writings of this remarkable Christian. Eckhart's works are presented in more complete and scholarly form elsewhere. Here, however, is a start. It is an amazing journey for any Christian. Meister Eckhart takes us on no mere philosophical expedition, but on a journey into God.

Halcyon Backhouse
Crostwight 1991

PART I

SERMONS

1

THE BIRTH OF JESUS

'Where is the one who has been born king of the Jews?'
(Matt. 2:2).

Now note where this birth occurs. I say again, as I have
often said before, that this birth falls in the soul exactly as
it does in eternity, neither more nor less, for it is the same
birth. This birth falls in the ground and essence of the
soul.

Certain questions, then, arise. Given that God is in all
things as intelligence (or mind), and is more innate and
natural in things than things are in themselves, and given
that God is at work no matter where he is, knowing himself and speaking his Word, given these things, then note
in what respects the soul is better fitted for this divine
work than other rational creatures in which God works.

God is in all things as being, as activity, as power. But
God gives birth in the soul alone, for though every creature bears God's mark, the soul is the natural image of
God. This image is perfected and adorned in this birth. No
creature but the soul alone is susceptible to this act, this
birth. Whatever perfection enters the soul, whether it be
divine light, grace or bliss, must enter the soul in this
birth. There is no other way. If you nurture this birth in
yourself, you will experience all good, all comfort, all

happiness, all being and all truth. Whatever comes to you in this way brings true being, and stability. Whatever else you may seek and grasp without this, it will perish, no matter how you possess it. This alone gives life; all else corrupts. And further, through this birth you participate in the divine influx and its gifts. They are not received by creatures in whom God's image is not found. The idea of the soul belongs to the eternal birth alone, and this happens only and solely in the soul. It is born of the Father in the ground and innermost recesses of the soul where no image gleamed or power of the soul peeped.

Thus another question is: If this birth falls in the ground and essence of the soul, then it happens to saint and sinner alike, so what good or use is it to me? Nature's ground is the same in both, and even in hell the nobility of nature persists eternally.

It is characteristic of this birth that it always comes with fresh light. It always brings great enlightenment to the soul because it is the nature of good to spread outwards. In this birth God pours into the soul such a huge amount of light, and the ground and essence of the soul are so flooded with it, that it runs over into all her powers, flowing into the outward self as well.

This is what happened to Paul on his journey when God touched him with his light and spoke to him. Paul's companions saw the reflection of this light as it showed itself outwardly, surrounding Paul like the saints. The superabundance of light in the ground of the soul overflows into the body, which is filled with radiance.

No sinner can receive this light, nor is he worthy to. He is full of sin, wickedness and darkness. As John says, 'The darkness has not understood it' (John 1:5). In the sinner the paths through which light enters are blocked and obstructed with deceit and darkness. Light and darkness are incompatible, like God and creatures. Enter God, exit creatures. Man is quite conscious of this light. Directly he turns to God, it begins to glint and sparkle in him. It tells him what to do and what to leave undone, with many a shrewd hint, moreover, about things he had previously ignored or knew nothing of.

How do you know?

Suppose your heart is strongly inclined to retire from the world. How could that happen unless it were by this light? This light is so charming, so delightful, that everything else appears tiresome if it is not God or God's. It attracts you to God, and you are aware of many good impulses, even though you may be uncertain where they come from. This interior mood is in no way due to creatures, nor does it come at their bidding, for what creatures effect and direct comes in from outside. But your ground alone is stirred by this force, and the freer you are, the more truth and discernment are yours. No man was ever lost except for one reason: having once left his ground he has let himself become too permanently settled abroad. St Augustine says: 'There are many who have sought light and truth, but only abroad where they are not.' These people go out so far, finally, that they never get back nor find their way in again. They do not find the truth, for the truth is within, in their ground, and not outside. So anyone who seeks to see this light and find out the whole truth must foster the awareness of this birth within himself, in his ground. So his powers will be lit up, and his outer self as well. As soon as God inwardly stirs a man's ground with the truth, its light darts into his powers and that man knows more than anyone could teach him. As the prophet says, 'I know more than I was ever taught.' It is because this light cannot lighten and shine in sinners that this birth cannot occur in them. This birth is incompatible with darkness and sin, and therefore it does not fall in the powers but in the ground and essence of the soul.

Then the question comes: If God the Father labours only in the ground and essence of the soul, not in her powers, what have the powers got to do with it? How do they help by being idle and taking a holiday? What is the use, seeing that this birth falls outside the powers?

A good question. But think. Every creature works towards some end. The end is always the first in intention and the last in execution. So, too, God works for a wholly blessed end, namely, himself: to bring the soul and all her powers into that end, into himself. For this God's works are wrought, for this the Father brings his Son to birth in the soul, so that all the powers of the soul may end in this. He lies in wait for all the soul contains; all are invited to his royal feast. Here, the soul is scattered abroad among her powers and dissipated in the act of each: the power of seeing in the eye, the power of hearing in the ear, the power of tasting in the tongue.The soul's powers are accordingly weakened for their interior work, because scattered forces are imperfect. It follows that the soul must call in all her powers if her interior work is to be effective. She must collect them together out of exterior things into one interior act. St Augustine says: 'The soul is where she loves rather than where she animates the body.'

Once upon a time there was a heathen philosopher who studied mathematics. He was sitting by his fire making calculations when a man came along brandishing a sword. Not realising it was the master, he cried, 'Quick, your name or I slay you.' The master was far too absorbed to see or hear his enemy, and failed to catch the threat. After warning him several times, the enemy cut off his head. And all that just to acquire a mere natural science! How much more ready we should be to withdraw from things in order to concentrate our powers on perceiving and knowing the one infinite and immortal truth! To this end, then, assemble your entire mind and memory: turn them into the ground where your treasures lie hidden. Yet for this you must drop all other activities. You must get to unknowing to find it.

The question is: Would it not be better for each power to go on with its own work, then none of them would hinder the others in their work, nor God in his work? Can there not be creaturely knowledge in me that is no hindrance, as God knows all things without hindrance, and so do the saints?

My answer: The saints look upon God in a simple image, and in that image they see everything. God, too, sees himself in this way, perceiving all things in himself. He need not turn, as we do, from one thing to another. Suppose we were to see everything in this life in a mirror in which everything is recognised at a glance, in one single image: neither action nor knowledge would be a hindrance then. But now we must turn from one thing to the next: we can only keep in mind one thing at the expense of others. And the soul is so tightly bound to her powers that where they go she goes too. The soul must be present wherever the powers are in action, and must pay attention, or nothing would come of their exertions. This drain of attending to her external acts is bound to weaken her interior working.

For his nativity God wants, and must have, a vacant, free and unencumbered soul where there is nothing but himself alone, which waits for nothing and no one but God alone. As Christ says, 'Whoever loves anything else but me, whoever clings to father, mother or many other things, is not worthy of me. I came on earth not to bring peace, but a sword; to cut away all things, to part you from brother, child, mother, and friend, which are really your foes' (see Matt. 10:34-37). For truly your comforts are your foes. Does your eye see all things, your ear hear all things, and your heart remember all things? Then in these things your soul is destroyed.

A master says, 'To achieve the interior act, one must assemble all one's powers, as it were, into one corner of one's soul, where, secreted from images and forms, one is able to work. We must sink into oblivion and ignorance. In this silence, this quiet, the Word is heard. There is no better method of approaching this Word than in silence, in

quiet: we hear it and know it aright in unknowing. To one
who knows nothing, it is clearly revealed.'

You may perhaps object: 'Sir, you place our salvation in
ignorance. That seems mistaken. God made man to know,
as the prophet says, "Lord, make them know." Where
ignorance remains, there is defect and illusion; one
remains brutish, an ape, a fool, as long as one is ignorant.'

But I am speaking of transformed knowledge, not
ignorance that comes from lack of knowing; it is by knowing that we get to this unknowing. Then we know with
divine knowing, then our ignorance is ennobled and
adorned with supernatural knowledge. Then in our passion we are more perfect than in action. According to one
authority, the sense of hearing is much nobler than the
sense of sight. For we learn wisdom more through the ear
than the eye, and live this life more wisely.

We read about a heathen philosopher who was lying at
death's door while his pupils were discussing some noble
science in his presence. Lifting up his dying head to hear,
he exclaimed, 'O teach me even now this art, that I may
practise it eternally!'

Hearing draws in more, seeing leads out more. In eternal life we are far more happy in our ability to hear than in
our power to see, because the act of hearing the eternal
Word is in me, whereas the act of seeing goes out from
me. Hearing, I am receptive; seeing, I am active. Yet our
bliss does not consist in being active but in being receptive
to God. As God excels his creatures, so God's work excels
mine. It was out of love that God set our happiness in suffering, for we undergo far more than we do, and receive
incomparably more than we give in return. Each divine
gift is the preparation for some new and richer gift, each
gift increasing our capacity and desire to receive one
greater still. Some theologians say that the soul is symmet-
rical with God in this respect. For as God is infinite in giving, so the soul is infinite in receiving or conceiving. The
soul can suffer profoundly, just as God can act omnipo-

tently, and so the soul is transformed by God into God. God must act and the soul must suffer, for him to know and love himself in her, and for her to know with his knowledge, love with his love. Since she is far happier in his than hers, it follows that her happiness depends upon his work more than on her own.

Dionysius' pupils asked him why Timothy outstripped them in perfection. Dionysius said, 'Timothy is a God-receptive man. The one expert in this outstrips all men.' In this sense your unknowing is not a defect, but your chief perfection, and your suffering your highest activity. Kill your activities and still your powers if you would realise this birth in yourself. To find the newborn King in you, all else you might find must be passed by and left behind. May we outstrip and leave behind those things that are not pleasing to the newborn King. So help us, Jesus, who became the child of man that we might become the children of God. Amen.

2

MY FATHER'S BUSINESS

'I must be about my Father's business' (Luke 2:49, AV).

This text is pertinent to what we have been saying about the eternal birth. It took place here in time and is still happening daily in the innermost recesses of the soul, in her ground, remote from all comers. To become aware of this interior birth it is above all necessary to be about our Father's business.

What is peculiarly the Father's? Power is ascribed to him beyond that ascribed to either of the other Persons. And I tell you, no one can experience this birth without a mighty effort. No one can attain this birth unless he can withdraw his mind entirely from things. It requires great force to drive back all the senses and inhibit them. Violence must be directed to each one or this cannot happen. As Christ said: 'The kingdom of heaven has been forcefully advancing, and forceful men lay hold of it' (Matt. 11:12).

Now a question arises over this birth. Does it happen continuously, or only at intervals when one is disposed for it and exerting oneself to the utmost to forget everything else completely and be conscious only of this?

Here let us distinguish. Man possesses an active intellect, a passive intellect and a potential intellect. The active intellect is ever in action, ever doing something, either in God or

20

in the creature, to the honour and glory of God. That is its province, and hence its name, active. But when God undertakes the work, the mind must preserve a state of passivity.

The potential intellect has regard to both these, to the action of God and the passivity of the soul. In one case the mind is active, when it is functioning; in the other receptive, when God takes up the work. Then the mind ought, in fact must, remain still and allow God to act. Now before this is begun by the mind and finished by God, the spirit foresees it, it has potential knowledge of its happening. This is what is meant by potential intellect. It is, however, often neglected and does not bear fruit.

When the mind is exerting itself in real earnest, God involves himself in the mind and its work. Then the soul sees and experiences God. But since the uninterrupted vision and experience of God is intolerable to the soul in this body, from time to time God withdraws from the soul, as it is said, 'In a little while you will see me no more, and then after a little while you will see me' (John 16:16).

Our Lord took his three disciples with him up the mountain and showed them the transfiguration of his body by union with the Godhead – a transfiguration which we will also have in our archetypal body – and as he looked upon it, Peter at once wished to remain there always. Truly, where we find good we are loath to leave it. Where intuition finds, love follows, and memory and all the soul as well. And knowing this, our Lord hides himself sometimes, for the soul, being the indivisible form of the body, turns as a whole to whatever she turns. If she were conscious of good, that is, of God, immediately, uninterruptedly, she would never be able to leave it to influence the body. This is what happened with Paul. Had he remained a hundred years there, where he knew the good, he would never have returned to his body, he would have forgotten it completely.

Seeing, then, that the good is wholly foreign to this life,

and incompatible with it, the good God veils it when he
wishes, and unveils it again when he so chooses and
when he knows, like a good doctor, that it is best and
most useful for you. This withdrawal is not of your making, but his, as is also the work. Let him do it or not
as he wills, for he knows what is good for you. It is in
his hands to reveal himself or not as you are able to
endure it. God is not a destroyer of nature; he perfects
it. And God does this more and more, as you are fitted
for it.

Perhaps you will object and say, 'Unfortunately, sir, if
this requires a mind quite free from images and without
activity, though both are natural to its powers, then how
about those outward works we must do sometimes? I am
referring to works of charity, external acts, such as teaching and comforting those in need of comfort. Are we bar-
red from doing these things which so occupied our Lord's
disciples, especially St Paul, who experienced a father's
care for other people? Are we to be deprived of the great
good you have been talking about because we are engaged
in charitable works?'

The answer is this. The one is perfect, the other very
profitable. Mary was praised for choosing the best, but
Martha's life serving Christ and his disciples was very useful. St Thomas says the active life is better than the life of
contemplation when we actually spend in charitable work
the income we derive from contemplation. Then it is all
the same thing. We have only to root ourselves in this
same ground of contemplation to make it fruitful in works,
and the object of contemplation is achieved. True, there is
motion, but only one. It comes from one end, God, and
goes back to God. It is as if I went from one end of this
house to the other end: it is true that it would be motion,
but of one in the same. Even so, in this activity we are in
the state of contemplation in God. The one activity is
centred in the other and perfects the other. God's purpose
in the union of contemplation is fruitfulness in works. In

contemplation you serve yourself alone, but in good works you serve many.

In this respect, Christ instructs us by his whole life and the lives of all his saints, every one of whom he led out into the world to teach the multitude. St Paul said to Timothy, 'Preach the Word' (2 Tim. 4:2). Did he mean the outward word that beats the air? Surely not! He meant the in-born, hidden Word that lies secretly in the soul. It was this that he exhorted them to preach, so that it might be made known to and nourish the powers of those who spend themselves wholly in the exterior life. This is so that whenever your fellow man is in need of you, you may be found ready to serve him to the best of your ability. It must be within you, in thought, in intellect and will, and shine out in your actions. When Christ said, 'Let your light shine before men' (Matt. 5:16), he was thinking of those people who care only for the contemplative life and neglect the virtuous uses of it, which, they say, do not concern them because they have passed that stage. Christ did not have these people in mind when he observed: 'Other seed fell on good soil. It came up, grew and produced a crop, multiplying thirty, sixty, or even a hundred times' (Mark 4:8). But he was referring to them when he declared: 'Every tree that does not produce good fruit will be cut down' (Matt. 3:10).

You may object: 'But, sir, what of that silence you said so much about? This fruitful work means images galore. Every one of these acts has its appropriate image, be the act internal or external, teaching one person or comforting another, arranging this or that. What quiet is there in all this? If the mind sees and formulates and the will wills and memory holds it fast, does not all this necessitate ideas?'

Let me explain. We were speaking just now of the active intellect and the passive intellect. The active intellect abstracts the essential images, stripping them of outward material things and non-essentials. Then it introduces them to the passive intellect, where their mental prototypes originate. And the passive intellect, made pregnant by the active in this way, knows and cherishes these things with the help of the active intellect. The passive intellect cannot keep on knowing things unless the active intellect keeps on enlightening it. Now observe. What the active intellect does for the natural man, that, and far more, God does for the solitary soul. He turns out the active intellect, installing himself in its stead, and he himself assumes the duties of the active intellect.

When a man is quite idle, when his intellect is at rest within him, then God takes up the work: he himself is the agent who produces himself in the passive intellect. What happens is this. The active intellect cannot give what it has not got: it cannot have two ideas at the same time, but has first one idea and then another. Even though light and air show multitudes of forms and colours instantaneously, you can only observe them one after another. And that is how it is with your active intellect, which resembles the eye. But when God acts in place of your active intellect, he engenders many images together in one point. Suppose God prompts you to perform a good deed for someone. At once your powers are all offered for all virtuous things, your mind being set on the general good. All your possibilities for good take shape and come into your mind collectively, all of them focused on one point. Clearly this is not the work of your own intellect, which has neither the perfection nor the richness for it. Rather, it is the work and product of him who has all forms at once in himself. As Paul says: 'I can do everything through him who gives me strength' (Phil. 4:13).

You must know, then, that the ideas of these acts are not your own: they belong to the author of your nature who has planted in you both their energy and form. Lay no claim to this, for it is his, not yours. True, you receive it temporally, but it is conceived and born of God beyond time, in eternity above images.

But you will perhaps say: 'When my intellect is divested

of its natural activity and no longer has either form or action of its own, what preserves it? It must have a hold somewhere. Its powers, whether memory, intellect or will, are bound to have some base somewhere, some place to work in.'

The answer is this. The intellect is sustained by essence, and not by outward events and activities: just pure unadulterated being in itself. Upon observing something real, the intellect at once relies upon it, it comes to rest on it, pronouncing its intellectual word concerning that object. As long as the intellect fails to find the actual truth of things, as long as it does not touch bedrock in them, it stays in a condition of quest and expectation. It never settles down to rest, but labours incessantly to trace things to their cause. It is seeking and waiting. It spends perhaps a year or more in research on some natural fact, finding out what it is, only to work as long again to strip off what it is not. All this time it has nothing to go by, it makes no pronouncement at all in the absence of experimental knowledge of the ground of truth.

Intellect never rests in this life. However much God shows himself in this life, it is nothing to what he really is. Truth lies in the ground, but is veiled and concealed from the intellect. And meanwhile the mind has no permanent support to rest on. It gets no rest at all, but goes on expecting and preparing for something still to come but so far hidden.

There is no knowing what God is. We do know something – what God is not. This the discerning soul rejects. Intellect, meantime, finding no satisfaction in any mortal thing, is waiting, as matter awaits form. As matter is insatiable for form, so intellect is satisfied only with the essential, all-embracing truth. Only the truth will do, and this God keeps withdrawing from it, step by step, purposing to arouse its zeal and lure it on to seek and grasp the actual causeless good. God's desire is that the soul, not content with any mortal thing, may clamour more and more for the highest good of all.

But you will say: 'Alas, sir, you laid so much stress on our quieting our powers, and now this calm resolves itself into yearning and lamenting, to moaning and clamouring for something not possessed, which puts an end to peace and quiet. This may be desire or purpose or praise or thanksgiving, or any of their brood, but it is not perfect peace and absolute stillness.'

I answer that when you have emptied yourself entirely of your own self and all things and of every sort of selfishness, and have transferred, united and abandoned yourself to God in perfect faith and complete friendship, then everything that is born in you or that enters into you, external or internal, joyful or sorrowful, sour or sweet, is no longer your own at all, but is altogether your God's to whom you have abandoned yourself. Tell me, whose is the spoken word? Is it his who speaks it or his who hears it? Though it falls to the hearer, it really belongs to the speaker, to the one who gave it birth. The sun, for example, throws out light into the air and the air receives the light and transmits it to the earth. Now, although the light seems to be in the air, it is really in the sun: the light is actually from the sun, originating in the sun, not in the air. The air merely entertains it and passes it on to anything that can be lit up.

And so with the soul. In the soul God gives birth to his child, his Word. Conceiving it, the soul passes it on to her powers in various guises, now as desire, now as good intentions, now as love, now as gratitude, or however it may take you. It is his, not yours at all. What is thus brought about by God you take as his and not your own. That is why it is written, 'The Spirit himself intercedes for us with groans that words cannot express' (Rom. 8:26). He prays in us, it is not we ourselves who are doing the praying. So St Paul says, 'No-one can say, "Jesus is Lord," except by the Holy Spirit' (1 Cor. 12:3).

Above all, lay no claim to anything. Let go of yourself and let God act for you and in you as he pleases. This work is his, this Word is his, this birth is his, and all you are as well. For you have abandoned yourself and have gone beyond your powers and your personal nature. God installs himself in your nature and powers when, having rid yourself of all belongings, you take to the desert, as it is written, 'A voice of one calling in the desert' (Matt. 3:3). Let this eternal voice cry on in you at its own sweet will while you are a desert in respect of self and creatures.

Maybe you will say: 'But, sir, what must one do to become this desert, empty of self and creatures? Should one stay waiting for God all the time and do nothing oneself, or should one do something in the meantime, such as praying or reading or some good occupation like going to church or studying the Bible? Not, of course, taking things in from without, but everything from within, from one's God. Besides, is there not something we miss if we neglect these things?'

My answer is this: Outward works were instituted and appointed for the purpose of directing the outer self to God and training him in the spiritual life and virtues, lest he should perhaps stray out of himself into foolishness. They were designed to act as a curb upon his inclination to run away from self to things outside; to ensure that when he chooses to work in him, God will find him close at hand and not first have to fetch him back from things gross and alien. The greater the pleasure in external things, the harder work it is to leave them; the stronger the love, the sharper the pain when it comes to parting.

All pious practices – praying, reading, singing, watching, fasting, penance, or whatever discipline it be – were contrived to protect and keep us from things alien and ungodly.

Suppose you feel that God's Spirit is not working in you, but rather that your inner self is God-forsaken, then that is the right moment for the outward self to exercise the practical virtues, particularly the ones that he finds most practicable and useful. This is not for his own selfish ends, but so that, as respect for truth preserves him from being led away by what is gross, he may stick strictly to God. Then God will not need to seek him far afield, but will find him there at hand when he chooses to return and carry on his own work in his soul.

But if a man has genuine experience of the interior life, then let him boldly drop all outward disciplines, even those practices to which he had committed himself and from which neither pope nor prelate could release him. From vows made to God no man can excuse you: such vows are a bond between yourself and God. But supposing you have taken solemn vows of fasting, say, or prayer or pilgrimage, then on entering some religious order you are at once released from them. In a monastery, obligation is to goodness as a whole, to God himself.

And so I say here. Whatever your vows may be to many external things, initiation into the real interior life releases you from them. As long as the interior experience lasts, whether it be a week, a month or a year, no hours are wasted by the monk or nun, for God who occupied them will also answer for them. On returning to himself, the religious will perform his vows for the present moment. But it is not his business to make up for the hours that have passed, and, as he sees it, have been lost. God makes good any time he takes up. Do not think that a creature must make up for lost time, for the smallest act of God outweighs all the work of creatures put together. I am speaking here of men in holy orders, and those enlightened souls who are illumined by God and by the Scriptures. But what about the layman who, ignorant of church discipline, has assumed some vow or other, praying or the like? My view is this. If he finds it hampering and discovers that he draws much closer to God and much more easily without it, let him boldly give it up, for whatever brings us nearest to God is the best. Paul implied this when he said: 'When perfection comes, the imperfect disappears' (1 Cor. 13:10).

Vows taken before priests, vows of marriage, for example, are very different from these other obligations which amount to solemn promises of oneself to God. Vows taken with the laudable intention of binding oneself to God are for the moment the best way. But supposing that we find a superior way, a way we feel and know to be much better, then the first may be deemed null and void.

3

THE ETERNAL BIRTH

'Today in the town of David a Saviour has been born to you; he is Christ the Lord' (Luke 2:11).

We read in the Gospel that when our Lord was twelve years old he went with Joseph and Mary to Jerusalem into the temple; and when they went out, Jesus remained behind in the temple without their knowing it. When they reached home and missed him, they searched for him among acquaintances and among strangers, among their relatives, and among the multitude, and did not find him. They had lost him in the crowd. So there was nothing for it but to retrace their steps, and when they got back to their starting-point, into the temple, there they found him.

If you truly wish to find this noble birth, you must leave the multitude and return to the starting-point, to the ground out of which you came. The powers of the soul and their works, these are the multitude. Memory, understanding and will all diversify you. Therefore you must leave them all: physical perception, imagination and everything in which you find yourself and see yourself. After this, you may find this birth, but, believe me, not otherwise. He has never been found among friends, nor among family nor acquaintances, rather, there one loses him altogether.

Now the question arises: Is this birth to be found in anything which, albeit relating to God, is nevertheless taken in from without, through the senses? Is it found in any appearance of God as good, wise, or compassionate, or in any other idea of divinity that the intellect may have? Is this birth to be found in any things like these?

In truth, no! Although good and godlike, they are nevertheless introduced from outside, through the senses. Everything must well up from within, out of God, if this birth is to shine with a really clear light. Your own work must be put on one side, and every faculty must serve his ends, not your own. If this work is to be done, God alone must do it, and you must undergo it. Where you go out from your own willing and knowing, God, with his knowing, surely and willingly goes in and shines there clearly. Where God thus knows himself, your knowledge is of no avail and cannot stand. Do not foolishly imagine that your reason can grow to the knowledge of God. No natural light can help to make God shine in you. Your own light must be utterly extinguished and be devoid of self completely, then God can shine in with his light, bringing back with him everything you left, and a thousand times more, as well as the new form containing it all.

This is illustrated in the Gospel. When our Lord had talked in such a friendly way with the Samaritan woman at the well, she left her water jar there, and running to the town announced that the true Messiah had come. Not believing her report, the people went out with her to see him for themselves. Then they said to her, 'We no longer believe just because of what you said; now we have heard for ourselves' (John 4:42).

Truly, you cannot be brought to know God divinely by any human science, nor by your own wisdom. To know God in God's way, your knowledge must change into outright unknowing, to a forgetting of yourself and every creature.

Now perhaps you will say: 'Well, sir, what is the use of

my intellect if it has to be inert and completely idle? Is my best plan really to raise my mind to the unknowing knowing which obviously cannot be anything, for if I knew anything it would not be ignorance, and I would not be idle and destitute? Must I remain in total darkness?'

Yes, indeed! You can do no better than take up your abode in total darkness and ignorance.

'Alas, sir! Must everything go then, and is there no return?'

No, truly! By rights there is no return.

'But what is this darkness? What does it mean, what is it called?'

It can only be called a potential receptivity, which, however, is not altogether lacking in (real) being: it is the merely potential conception in which you will be perfected. Hence there is no returning from it. If you return, it is not because of any truth, but because of the senses, the world or the devil. And if you persist in this turning back, you will inevitably lapse into sin and be likely to backslide so far that you fall for ever. Therefore, there is no turning back, only pressing forward and following up this possibility to its fulfilment. It never rests until fulfilled with all being. As matter never rests until fulfilled with every possible form, so intellect never rests till it is filled to all its capacity.

A heathen master says of this: 'Nature has nothing swifter than the heavens which surpass all else in swiftness.' But surely the mind of man outstrips them. If it retains its vigour and is not demeaned and torn apart by what is base and gross, it can outstrip high heaven and never slacken its pace till it gains the summit, where it is fed and cherished by the Arch-Good, by God himself.

How profitable it is, then, to pursue this goal, for by keeping yourself empty and bare, merely tracking and following and giving up yourself to this darkness and ignorance, without turning back, you may well win that which is all things. And the more barren you are in yourself, and ignorant of things, the nearer you are to it.

Of this barrenness it is written in Hosea: 'I will lead her into the desert and speak tenderly to her' (Hos. 2:14). The genuine Word of eternity is spoken only in eternity, where man is a desert and alien to himself and to multiplicity. For this desolate self-estrangement the prophet longed, saying: 'Oh, that I had the wings of a dove! I would fly away and be at rest!' (Ps. 55:6). Where shall I find peace and rest? Truly, in rejection, in desolation and estrangement from all creatures. Therefore David says: 'I would rather be a doorkeeper in the house of my God than dwell in the tents of the wicked' (Ps. 84:10).

Now perhaps you will say: 'Ah, sir, is it really necessary to be barren and estranged from everything, outward and inward? Must the powers and their works all go? It is very hard for a man to be left by God without support like this, and for God to increase his misery, neither enlightening him, nor encouraging him, nor working in him. For that is what your teaching means. When a person is in such downright nothingness, would it not be better for him to be doing something to ease the gloom and desolation: to pray or read or go to church, or else cope with it by working at some useful occupation?'

No, be sure of this: absolute stillness, absolute idleness is the best way of all. You cannot exchange this state for any other whatsoever without harming yourself. Much as you would like partially to fit yourself for it, and to let God partially fit you, that cannot be. No matter how quick you were to think of what is fitting, and to desire it, God would always forestall you. But granting the impossible – granting that this work could be shared, that the preparation for God's working or infusion in you could be jointly God's and yours – you must know that God is bound to act, to pour himself out into you as soon as ever he finds you ready. Don't think that God is like a human carpenter, who works or doesn't work as he chooses, who can do his work or leave it undone as the mood takes him. It is not like that with God. When he finds you ready, he is obliged to act, to flow into you, just as the sun must shine out and is unable to stop itself whenever the air is bright and clear. It would be a very grave defect indeed in God if, finding you so empty and so bare, he did not do any excellent work in you and did not fill you with glorious gifts.

Philosophers declare that the instant the embryo is ready in the mother's womb, into its body God pours its living spirit, that is, the soul, the form of the body. It happens in one flash: the being ready and the pouring in. In the same way, as nature reaches her peak, God dispenses his grace. The instant the spirit is ready, God enters in without hesitation or delay.

In the Revelation of St John it is written that our Lord offers himself to men: 'Here I am! I stand at the door and knock. If anyone hears my voice and opens the door, I will come in and eat with him, and he with me' (Rev. 3:20). You do not need to seek him here or there, he is no further off than the door of your heart. There he stands lingering, waiting for whoever is ready to open and let him in. You do not need to call to him in the distance. He is waiting much more impatiently than you, for you to open to him. He is longing for you a thousand times more urgently than you are for him. It is instantaneous: the opening and the entering.

You will perhaps say: 'How can that be? I have no inkling of him.'

It is not in your power to find him, but in his. He reveals himself when he chooses, and he hides himself, too, when he wills. This is what Christ meant when he said to Nicodemus, 'The wind blows wherever it pleases. You hear its sound, but you cannot tell where it comes from or where it is going' (John 3:8). This is a paradox: 'You hear its sound, but you cannot tell where it comes from.' Yet it is by hearing that we know. What Christ meant is that it is imbibed or absorbed through hearing, that is to say, you receive it unconsciously. God cannot leave anything void and unfilled. Nature's God cannot endure anything to be empty. If, therefore, you seem not to find him, and to be wholly empty of him, that is nevertheless not the case. For were there any emptiness under heaven, whatever it might be, however great or small, the heavens must either draw it up to them or, bending downwards, fill it with themselves. On no account will God, who is nature's Lord, permit anything to remain empty. Therefore stand still and do not waver, in case, turning away from God for a moment, you never turn back to him again.

Maybe you will say: 'Well, sir, since you are always assuming that some day this birth will happen in me, that the Son will be born in me, can I have any sign to help me recognise that it has taken place?'

Yes, to be sure! There will be three signs. I will tell you one of them. I am often asked whether it is possible to reach the point of not being hindered spiritually by anything in time, by any material object or any multiplicity. Indeed it is! If this birth really happens, nothing can hamper you, everything will point you to God and this birth. An analogy can be found in lightning. Lightning turns whatever it strikes – whether tree, beast or man – towards itself. A man with his back to it is instantly flung round to face it; all the thousand leaves of the tree turn over to face the lightning stroke. So it is with everyone who experiences this birth. Everything they encounter, be it never so earthly, immediately turns them towards it. Even what was previously a hindrance is now nothing but a help. Your face is turned so fully towards this birth that no matter what you see or hear, you receive nothing except this birth. All things are simply God to you, who see only God in all things. You are like someone who looks for quite a while at the sun, and afterwards sees the sun in whatever he looks at. If this is lacking in you, this looking for and seeing God in all and sundry, then you lack this birth.

You may question me: 'Ought anyone in this position to

undertake penances? Does he lose anything by dropping
penitential exercises?'

Penitential practices, among other things, were instituted for a special object. Fasting, watching, praying,
kneeling, scourging, wearing hair shirts, sleeping on a
hard surface, or whatever it may be, were all invented
because body and flesh are always in opposition to spirit.
Since the body is always far too strong for the spirit, battle
is always joined between them, it is a never-ending con-
flict. Here the body is bold and strong, for here it is at
home; the world helps it, the earth is its fatherland. It is
aided by all its family: food, drink, ease – all are opposed
to spirit. The spirit is an alien here. Its family, its whole
race, are in heaven; there its loved ones dwell. To aid the
spirit in its distress, and to impede the flesh slightly in this
battle, and prevent it conquering the spirit, we put the
bridle of penitential practices on to it. These help to curb
the flesh, so that the spirit may control it. This is done to
bring it into subjection. But it is a thousand times more
effective to put the bridle of love on it. With love you
overcome it most surely, with love you load it most heav-
ily.

God lies in wait for us, therefore, with nothing so much
as with love. For love is like the fisherman's hook. No fish
comes to the fisherman that is not caught on his hook.
Once it takes the hook, the fish is forfeit to the fisherman.
In vain it twists hither and thither – the fisherman is certain of his catch. And so I say of love: the one who is
caught by it is bound by the strongest of all bonds – and
yet it is a pleasant burden. The one who bears this sweet
burden travels further and gets nearer his goal than if he
submitted to any conceivable harshness. Moreover, he can
cheerfully put up with whatever falls, and cheerfully suffer
whatever God inflicts.

Nothing makes you so much God's, nor God so much
yours, as this sweet bond. The one who has found this way
will seek no other. The one who hangs on this hook is

caught so fast that foot and hand, mouth, eyes and heart and all that are his are bound to be God's.

There is, then, no better way to win over your enemy, and stop him harming you, than the way of love. Therefore it is written: 'Love is as strong as death, its jealousy as unyielding as the grave' (Song 8:6). Death separates soul from body, but love separates all things from the soul; not at any cost will she tolerate what is not God nor God's. Whoever is caught in this net, whoever walks in this way, will find that whatever he does, is done by love, whose alone the work is. It matters nothing whether he be busy or idle. His most trivial action is more profitable, his meanest occupation is more fruitful to himself and other people, and is more pleasing to God, than the cumulative works of other men, who, though free from mortal sin, are nevertheless inferior to him in love. He rests more usefully than others work.

Wait, therefore, for this hook, so you may be happily caught. And the more surely caught, the more surely you will be freed.

That we may be thus caught and freed, help us, O you who are love itself. Amen.

4

GOD IS LOVE

'God is love. Whoever lives in love lives in God, and God in him' (1 John 4:16).

This is from the epistle we read at Mass, and it is St John speaking.

Take the opening words: 'God is love.' Yes – in that by his love he compels all who can love and all who do love to love him. Secondly, God is love in that every God-created and loving thing compels him by its love to love it, willy-nilly. Thirdly, God is love in that his love drives all his lovers out of multiplicity. The love of God in multiplicity pursues the love which is himself right out of multiplicity into his very unity. Fourthly, God is love who, by his love, provides all creatures with their life and being, preserving them in his love. Just as the colour of cloth is preserved in the cloth, so creatures are preserved in existence by love, that is, God. Take the colour from cloth, and its being is gone; so creatures all lose their being if taken from love, that is, from God. God is love, and so lovely is he that lovers all love him, willy-nilly. No creature is so vile that it loves what is bad. What we love must be good or must seem to be good. But creaturely good, all told, is rank evil compared with God. St Augustine says, 'Love, that in meditating love you may provide the means to satisfy your soul.' God is love.

My children, pay attention to me, I beg. Know this. God loves my soul so much that whether he wishes it or not, his very life and being depend upon his loving me. To stop God loving me would be to rob him of his Godhood, for God is love no less than he is truth. As he is good, so he is love as well. This is the absolute truth, as God lives.

Certain theologians maintained that the love which is within us is the Holy Spirit, but this is false. The physical food we take is changed into us, but the spiritual food we receive changes us into itself. Divine love is not preserved in us, otherwise there would be two. Divine love preserves us in itself as one in the same.

'God is love. Whoever lives in love lives in God, and God in him.' There is a difference between spiritual things and physical things. One spiritual thing dwells in another; but nothing physical dwells in another. There may be water in a tub, with the tub round it. But where the wood is, the water is not. In this sense, no material thing dwells in another. But spiritual things dwell in each other: each angel with all his joy and happiness is in every other angel as well as in himself, and every angel with all his joy and happiness dwells in me, and God as well with his supreme happiness, even if I do not discern it.

If anyone were to ask me what God is, I would answer: God is love, and so altogether lovely that creatures are all united to seek to love his loveliness, whether they do so knowingly or unbeknown to themselves, in joy or sorrow. Take, for instance, the lowest angel in his pure nature: the smallest spark or love-light that ever fell from him would light up the whole world with love and joy. See his innate perfection! Moreover, as I have explained at various times, the angels are numerous beyond number.

But to leave love and come to knowledge. If only we knew God it would be easy to forsake the world. All that God ever made or will yet make, all this, I say, if God gave it to my soul without himself, and he stayed, so to speak, a hair's-breadth off, would not content my soul nor make me happy. I am happy when all things are in me and God, and where I am God is, and where God is I am.

'Whoever lives in love lives in God, and God in him.' Suppose I am in God, then where he is, I am; and if God is in me, then, unless the Scriptures lie, where I am, God is. It is the absolute truth, as God is God.

'Faithful servant, I will set you over all my goods' (see Matt. 24:47, AV), that is, I will set you over the manifold goodness of God in creatures. Secondly, 'I will set you over all my goods' means: at the source of creaturely happiness, in the pure unity of God himself in which he has his own happiness. In other words, God being the good, in that sense he will set us above his manifold goodness. Thirdly, he will set us over all his goods means above all that can be named, all that can be expressed in words, all so-called good things, and all that can be understood by the intelligence. Thus he sets us over all his goods.

'That all of them may be one, Father, just as you are in me and I am in you' (John 17:21). Where two grow into one, one loses its nature. Therefore, for God and the soul to be one, the soul has to lose her own life and nature. They are one as regards what is left. But for them to be one, one must lose its identity and the other must keep its identity. Then they are the same. Now, the Holy Spirit says: 'Let them be one as we are one' (John 17:22) – make them the same in us.

When I pray for ought, my prayer counts for naught; when I pray for naught, I pray as I ought. When I am one with that in which are all things, past, present and to come, all the same distance and all just the same, then they are all in God and all in me. There is no thought of Henry or of Conrad. Praying for aught save God alone is idolatry and unrighteousness. They pray aright who pray in spirit and in truth. When praying for someone, for Henry or Conrad, I pray at my weakest. When praying for no one I pray at my strongest, and when I want nothing and make no request I am praying my best, for in God there is no Henry and no Conrad. To pray to God for aught save God is wrong and faithless, and, is, as it were, an imperfection. For to set up something beside God is, as I said, only to make naught of God and God of naught. Whoever is as far from and as foreign to himself as is the chief angel of the Seraphim owns that same angel just as God does and is God, and that's the naked truth, as God is God. 'God is love. Whoever lives in love lives in God, and God in him.'

May all of us attain this love of which I speak. So help us, our Lord Jesus Christ. Amen.

5

INTO THE TEMPLE

'Jesus entered the temple area and drove out all who were buying and selling there' (Matt. 21:12).

We read in the Gospel that our Lord went into the temple and cast out all who were buying and selling. He said to the men selling doves: 'Take these things away!' It was his purpose to have the temple cleared, as though he said: 'This temple is mine by rights and I want it to myself to be Lord of it.'

This temple in which God means to rule is man's soul which he has made exactly like himself, as the Lord says: 'Let us make man in our image, in our likeness' (Gen. 1:26). And this he did. God made man's soul so like himself that nothing else in earth or heaven resembles God so closely as the human soul. God wants this temple cleared of everything but himself. This is because this temple is so agreeable to him and he is so comfortable in it when he is there alone.

Now consider who these people were who were selling and buying in the temple, and who they are still. Understand what I mean: I am talking only of the virtuous. Yet, even so, I can point out who the traders were, and still are to this day, who buy and sell like this – the ones whom our Lord drove out. He still casts out those who buy and sell in this temple: he will not leave a single one. Look at them, they are all of them traders. Though they avoid mortal sin and wish to be righteous, doing good works of the sort that glorify God – for example, fasts, vigils, prayers, etc. – all of which are excellent, they do them with a view to God giving them something, or doing something for them in return. All such people are traders. This is plain to see, for they reckon on giving one thing for another, and so they barter with our Lord. They are, however, mistaken about what they are doing, for all they have, and all they have the power to do, comes from God, and they are able to do it by means of God alone. There is no call on God to do anything for them or give them anything unless he so chooses. For what they are, they are from God, and what they have, they get from God, not from themselves. God is in no way bound to pay them back for their acts or gifts. If they do receive anything, it is because he cares to give it of his own free will, irrespective of what they do or give. For they are not giving what is theirs, nor are they acting from themselves. As God says, 'Apart from me you can do nothing' (John 15:5).

People who bargain with our Lord like this are poor fools; they know little or nothing of the truth. God cast them out of the temple and drove them away. For light and darkness cannot dwell together. God is the truth; he is the light itself. When God enters the temple he drives out ignorance and darkness, revealing himself in the light of truth. Traders go when the truth appears, for the truth needs no selling. God does not seek his own; he is perfectly free in all his acts, and he acts in true love. So does the man who is at one with God: he is perfectly free in all his deeds. He does them out of love and without question, just to glorify God, not seeking anything for himself. God energises him.

Moreover, I maintain that as long as we do any work at all for gain, as long as we desire anything God may have given or may give, we rank with these traders. Would you

be free from any taint of trading with God? Then do what
good you can, and do it solely for God's glory, as free
from it yourself as though you did not exist. Ask nothing
whatever in return. Done in this way, your works are
spiritual and godly. The traders are driven from the temple and God is there alone when one has no motive but
God. See your temple cleared of traders. The man who is
intent on God alone, and on God's glory, is truly free from
any taint of commerce in his deeds, nor is he self-seeking
in any way.

I have described how Jesus said to those who were selling doves: 'Take these things away!' He did not drive
these people out, nor rebuke them harshly. He said quite
mildly: 'Take these things away!' as though to say, it is not
wrong, albeit a hindrance to the pure and simple truth.
These are virtuous folk, working for God impersonally,
though subject to personal limitations – to time and
number, to what has gone before and will come after.
Their activities keep them from the highest truth, from
being absolutely free like our Lord Jesus Christ, who is
constantly and timelessly receiving himself anew from his
heavenly Father, and in that same instant is born back
again unceasingly with praise and thanksgiving into the
Father, perfect, equal with him in his majesty. Even so, to
be receptive to the sovereign truth, a man must be without
before and after, without the hindrance of any acts or
images that are within his ken. He must freely receive the
divine gift in the perennial now and carry it back unhindered, with praise and thanksgiving in our Lord Jesus
Christ. Then the doves are gone, that is, the obstacle of
actions, in which, though they are good in themselves, one
has any self-interest. 'Take these things away!' said our
Lord, as though to say, they are blameless but they are in
the way. When the temple is free from obstructions (possessions and strangers) it looks quite beautiful, shining out
bright and clear above everything God has created and
through everything God has created, so that nothing can

be compared with it but the uncreated God alone.

In very truth, nothing is like this temple but the un-created God himself. Nothing below the angels is the least like it. In many ways, the very highest angels are the same as this temple of the human soul, but not entirely. Their partial likeness with the soul lies in love and knowledge. But a limit is set which they cannot pass. The soul goes on beyond. Suppose the soul were identical with the highest human being here in time, nevertheless that man has the potential freedom to soar to untold heights above the angels in the now of each, new without number, that is, without mode: above the angelic mode and every created intelligence. God who alone is uncreated is the soul's only peer in freedom, though not in uncreatedness, for the soul is created. Emerging into the unclouded light she in her naught leaps so far into his naught that she is helpless to regain the state of her created aught. God with his uncreatedness supports her nothing-at-all, preserving the soul in his all-in-all. The soul has dared to come to naught and, failing by herself to reach herself, she swoons away before God comes to her rescue. That is how it must be.

Jesus, as I said, went into the temple and cast out those who bought and sold, and ordered the others, 'Take these things hence!' Observe, no one was there but Jesus when he began to speak in the temple of the soul. Be sure of this, while anyone else is speaking in the temple of the soul, Jesus is silent, as though he were away. Nor is he at home in the soul while she has strange guests to talk to. For Jesus to speak in the soul she must be all alone, and she has to be quiet to hear what he says.

Well then, he comes in and starts speaking. What is it he says? He says what he is. What is he, then? He is the Word of the Father. In Jesus the Father speaks himself, in all his divine nature, in all that God is, just as he knows it, and he knows it as it is, for he is perfect in knowledge and power. It follows that he is perfect in speech too. When he pro-nounces the Word, he utters himself and all things in another Person to whom he gives the nature that he has himself. And all intelligences echo the Word, according to the indwelling image. Like the sun's rays shining out, so each intelligence is a word in itself, though not the same in all respects as the Word. They have the power to receive by grace the same nature as the actual Word; and this entire Word as it is in itself the Father spoke by the Word and everything in that Word.

If this is what the Father said, then what is Jesus saying in the soul? As I have said, the Father speaks his Word; he speaks in this Word and nowhere else, and Jesus speaks in the soul. He speaks to reveal himself and what the Father said in him, as far as the soul is able to receive it. He reveals the Father in the soul in infinite power. As it experiences this power in the Son, the soul flows out from it and grows in power till she is the same in might and virtue and every perfection. Then neither joy nor sorrow nor anything that God has made in time can avail to destroy that soul. She stands firm in this divine power against which all else is insignificant and futile.

Secondly, Jesus reveals himself in the soul in infinite wisdom. That wisdom is himself, the wisdom in which the Father knows himself in full fatherly power. The very Word, which is wisdom itself, and all that is in it, is, at the same time, one alone. When wisdom is in union with the soul, doubt, error and illusion are entirely removed. She is set in the bright pure light of God himself, as the prophet says, 'In your light we see light' (Ps. 36:9). Then God is known by God in the soul. With his wisdom she discerns both herself and all things. She does not know this wisdom from herself, but with this wisdom she discerns the Father, fruitful in labour, and his real being, in indivisible oneness, empty of all distinctions.

Jesus also reveals himself in infinite delight and fullness in all receptive hearts. When Jesus reveals himself in this plenitude of sweetness, and unites with the soul, then on this happy tide the soul floats into herself and out of herself and beyond the things of grace, back in unmitigated power into her first source. Thus the outward self is obedient, even unto death, to the inner self, now established in peace in the service of God for ever.

May Jesus enter into us and clear out and cast away all hindrances of soul and body, to the end that we may be one with him here upon earth and there in heaven. So help us, God. Amen.

6

SONS OF GOD

'How great is the love the Father has lavished on us, that we should be called children of God!' (1 John 3:1).

It is all the same thing: knowing God and being known by God, and seeing God and being seen by him. We know God and see him because he makes us know and see. Even as the luminous air cannot be distinguished from its luminant, for it is luminous with what illumines it, so we know by being known, by his making us conscious. Christ said, 'I will see you again' (John 16:22). That is, by making you see I make you see me. At this, 'You will rejoice' (John 16:22), rejoice in the vision and knowledge of God, and 'no-one will take away your joy'.

St John says: 'Behold, what manner of love the Father hath bestowed upon us, that we should be called and should be the sons of God.' He says not only 'should be called' but 'should be'. Now I maintain that we can no more be wise without wisdom than sons without the filial nature of God's Son: without having the very same nature as the Son of God himself. Would you be the Son of God? You cannot, not without having the same nature as the Son of God. But this is hidden from us here, as it is written, 'Beloved, now are we the sons of God, and it doth not yet appear what we shall be: but we know that, when he

48

shall appear, we shall be like him' (1 John 3:2, AV) – that is, the same as he is, the same life and enjoyment and understanding, exactly the same as he is, when we see him as God.

God cannot make me the Son of God if I do not have the nature of God's Son, any more than he can make me wise without my having wisdom. Though we are God's sons, we do not realise it yet: 'it doth not yet appear' to us. But this much we do know, he says: 'we shall be like him'. Various things in our souls cover over this knowledge and conceal it from us.

The soul has something in her, a spark of intellect, that never dies; and in this spark, as at the apex of the mind, we place the pattern of the soul. In our souls also there is knowledge of external things, physical and rational perception. They are present there as images and words which obscure the soul from us. How are we God's sons? By having one nature with him. But any realisation of this, of being God's sons, is subjective not objective knowledge. The inner consciousness strikes down to the very essence of the soul. Not that it is the soul itself, but it is rooted there and is in a measure the life of the soul, her intellectual life, the life, that is, in which a man is born God's son, born into the eternal life, for this knowledge is timeless, unextended, without here and without now. In this life all things are the same thing and all things are held in common; all things are all in all, and all are one.

I will give you an illustration. In the body the members are united so that the eye belongs to the foot and the foot to the eye. If the foot could speak, it would declare that the eye seems rather to be in the foot than in the head, and the eye would say the same the other way round. Accordingly, I believe that the grace which is in Mary is really more an angel's, and is more in him (yet being in Mary) than if it were in him or in the saints. For everything that Mary has belongs to every saint, so the grace in Mary is his own and he enjoys it more than if it really were in him.

But such a simile is too gross and carnal, depending as it does on bodily imagery. I will give you another, therefore, that is more subtle and less material. I assert that in heaven all is in all and all is one and all is ours. The grace our Lady has exists in me (when I am there), not welling up in and flowing out of Mary, but in me, my own and not of foreign origin. I contend that in that place, what one has another has, not from another nor in another, but in its own self, so that the grace in one is simultaneously in another as his own grace. Thus, spirit is in spirit. And that is why I cannot be the son of God unless I have the very nature the Son of God has. It is having the same nature that makes us the same. 'But it doth not yet appear what we shall be.' I take this to mean that there are no such things as 'like' or 'different', but that wholly without distinction we are the same in essence and in substance and in nature as he is himself. This is not apparent now: it will be obvious when we see him as God.

God makes us know him, and his knowing is his being, and his making me know is the same as my knowing. So his knowing is mine, just as, in the case of a teacher, what he teaches and what the pupil is taught are the same. And because God's knowing is mine, and his knowing is his substance and his nature and his essence, it follows that his substance and his nature and his essence are mine. And his substance, his nature and his essence being mine, I am the Son of God. 'Behold, what manner of love the Father hath bestowed upon us, that we should be called the sons of God.'

Note how we are the sons of God: by having the same nature as the Son of God. But how can someone be the Son of God, or know it, if that God is not like anybody?

True, Isaiah says, 'To whom, then, will you compare God? What image will you compare him to?' (Isa. 40:18). Since it is God's nature not to be like anyone, to be the same as he is, we must not be like anyone. When I contrive to see myself in naught and to see naught in me; when

I succeed in rooting up and casting out everything in me, then I am free to pass into the naked being of the soul. Likenesses must be ousted before I can be transplanted into God and be the same as he is: the same substance, the same essence, the same nature and the Son of God. Once this happens, there is nothing hidden in God that is not revealed, that is not mine. I am wise and mighty, just as he is, and one and the same with him. Then Sion is a true beholder, true Israel, a seer. He is God, since nothing in the Godhead is concealed from him. Man is turned into God. But in order that nothing may be concealed from me, and everything revealed, there must be no likeness, no image in me, for God's nature and his essence cannot be shown by any image. While any image or likeness dwells in you, you can never be the same as God. To be the same as God, there must be nothing in you, latent or defined, nothing covered in you that is not discovered and cast out.

Notice what sin is. It is born of negation. Negation's brood must be exterminated in the soul. While there is 'not' in you, you are not the Son of God. We weep and lament because we lack something. The minus quantity must go, it must be cancelled out, if man is to become the Son of God and weep and wail no more. Man is not wood or stone, imperfection and naught. We shall not be like God until this minus is made good and we are all in all as God is all in all.

Man has two births: one in the world, the other one out of the world and spiritual, in God. Do you wish to know if your child is born and if he is naked – that is to say, whether you have been made God's son? If your heart is heavy, for any reason other than sin, your child is not born. In your anguish you are not yet a mother: you are in labour and your hour is near. Do not doubt it: if you are labouring for yourself or for your friend, no birth has taken place, though birth is close at hand. The birth is not over till your heart is free from care. Then man has the essence and nature and substance and wisdom and joy and all that God has. Then the very being of the Son of God is ours and in us, and we attain to actual deity.

Christ says, 'If anyone would come after me, he must deny himself and take up his cross and follow me' (Matt. 16:24). That is: cast away care and let perpetual joy reign in your heart. Thus the child is born. And when the child is born in me, the sight of friends or of father dead before my eyes will leave my heart untouched. If my heart were moved, the child would not be born in me, though its birth could be close. I maintain that God and his angels take such keen delight in every act a good man does that there is no joy like it. And accordingly, I say, the birth of this child in you gives you the keenest delight, a continuous, never-ending joy, in all good deeds. Hence the words: 'No-one will take away your joy' (John 16:22).

When I am transported into God, then God is mine and all he has. 'I am the Lord your God,' he says. Then I have real delight which neither pain nor sorrow can take from me, for then I am installed in God, where sorrow has no place. I will see that in God there is no anger nor sadness, but only love and joy. Though he sometimes seems to be angry with sinners, it is not really wrath, it is his kindness, the effect of his great love: 'The Lord disciplines those he loves' (Heb. 12:6). For the Holy Spirit is love. God's anger springs from love; he rebukes us without anger.

When nothing is grievous or hard, when all is pure joy, then truly your child is born. Strive to ensure that this child is not merely ready to be born, but is actually born in you, even as God's Son is always being born in God and is always born. May this come about, so help us God. Amen.

7

IN THIS WAS LOVE

'This is how God showed his love among us: He sent his one and only Son into the world that we might live through him' (1 John 4:9), that is, 'in and through the Son'.

Those who do not live through the Son are truly mistaken.

If a mighty king had a beautiful daughter and gave her to a poor man's son, every member of that man's family would rise in rank and be ennobled. Thus one learned doctor says, 'By God becoming man the whole human race has been ennobled and exalted. Therefore it is incumbent upon us to rejoice greatly that Christ our brother has with special power ascended up above the choir of angels and sits on the right hand of the Father.' This is well said, though I set little store by it. What profit is it to me that my brother is rich if I am poor, or wise if I am a fool?

I am saying something more than this, and of greater significance: God not only became man, he assumed human nature. Doctors agree that by nature all men are of equal rank. But I make bold to say that every good thing possessed by the saints and by Mary, God's mother, and Christ in his human nature, is also mine in this same nature.

Perhaps you will ask me: 'If in my nature I already possess all that Christ did in his humanity, why do we give Christ such a high position, and honour him as our Lord and God?'

We do it because he was a messenger from God to us, bringing us our happiness. The happiness he brought us was our own. When the Father gives birth to his Son in the innermost ground, what moves there has this nature. This same nature is one and indivisible. Anything distinct in it, or connected with it, is not it.

I want to make another, even harder, point. To subsist here and now in this pure nature a man must be so completely dead to himself that he wills as much good for someone across the seas whom his eyes have never seen as he does for himself. While you still wish better for yourself than for that man whom you have never seen you have missed the mark, nor have you even for an instant seen into this true ground. Perhaps in some far-fetched symbol you have beheld the truth as in an image, but it was not the best.

Secondly, you must be pure in heart; and only that heart is pure which has exterminated creaturehood.

And thirdly, you must be free from 'not'.

The question is asked: 'What burns in hell?' Doctors reply with one accord: 'self-will'. But I maintain: 'not' burns in hell. Suppose I take a burning coal and put it on my hand. If I then say the coal is burning me, I do it a great injustice. To define precisely what it is that burns me: 'not' does, because the coal has in it something my hand has not. You see, it is this 'not' that burns me. If my hand contained what the coal is and can provide, it would possess the fire-nature. In which case, all the fire that ever burned might be taken and heaped upon my hand without burning me. Likewise, I assert that God and those who are approaching God have in themselves something pertaining to real happiness which those who are apart from God have not, and therefore I maintain that it is this 'not' alone that torments the souls in hell more than self-will or any fire whatsoever. In truth I say, as far as 'not' is part of you, so far you are imperfect. To be perfect, then, you must be free from 'not'.

Further, my text says: 'For God so loved the world that he gave his one and only Son' (John 3:16). By this we understand not the external world, but the inner world. As surely as the Father, by his one nature, gives birth to the Son innately, so surely he gives birth to him in the innermost recesses of the mind, which is the inner world. Here God's ground is my ground, and my ground God's ground. Here I live in my own as God lives in his own. To one who even for an instant has seen into this ground, a thousand ducats of red beaten gold are worth no more than a false farthing. Out of this innermost ground your works should be wrought without question. Indeed, I maintain that as long as you do your works because of the kingdom of heaven, or God, or your own eternal happiness, that is to say, from outside you, all is not well with you. It may be tolerable, but it is not the best. Anyone who foolishly imagines that he will get more of God in thoughts, prayers, pious offices and so on, than by the fireside or in the market-place, in truth, merely takes God, as it were, and wraps his head in a cloak and hides him under the table. For anyone who seeks God under fixed forms lays hold of the form while missing the God concealed in it. But anyone who seeks God in no special guise lays hold of him as he is in himself. Such a person 'lives with the Son' and is the life itself. We might question life for a thousand years: 'Why do you live?' It would only say, if it replied at all, 'I live because I live.' For life lives in a ground of its own, it wells up out of its own. It lives without a cause, for it lives itself. And if anyone asked a proper man, one who works his own ground, 'Why do you work?' he too would say, if he told the truth: 'I work because I work.'

Where the creature stops, there God begins. All God

wants of you is for you to go out of yourself in respect of your creatureliness and let God be God in you. The smallest of creaturely images that ever takes shape in you is as big as God.

'How so?' you ask.

It is because it shuts out the whole of God. As soon as this image appears, God disappears with all his Godhood. As this image fades out God comes in. [No matter how godly a temporal image may be, it harms the soul three times over. First, it vexes spirituality; next, it tarnishes the soul's purity; and thirdly, it disturbs her detachment.

'What does God do to my mind?'

Transcend yourself and repress creatures: God does that to your mind.]

God longs for you to go out of yourself in respect of your creaturely nature. He longs for this as urgently as if his whole happiness depended on it. What can be the harm of letting God be God in you? Go clean out of yourself for God's sake, and God will go clean out of himself for your sake. Both being gone out, what remains is simply the one. In this one the Father gives birth to his Son, in his innermost source. From there the Holy Spirit blossoms, and there the will belonging to the soul originates in God. As long as this will remains unmoved by creatures and by creaturehood, it is free. Christ says: 'No-one has ever gone into heaven except the one who came from heaven' (John 3:13). Things are all made from nothing; hence their true source is nothing. As far as it inclines towards creatures, this noble will lapses into nothing with them.

The question is: Does the will lapse so far that it is never able to return? With one accord, doctors reply that it does not make up anything it has lost. But I maintain that if this will turns back, even for an instant, from its own self and created things and rallies to its source, there, in its own free origin, the will is free and in this instant lost time is all recovered.

People often say to me: 'Pray for me.' And I think to myself: 'Why ever do you go out? Why not stop at home and mind your own treasure? For indeed the whole truth is in you.'

May we be ready to stay thus in ourselves and to possess the entire truth immediately, without division, in real happiness. So help us God! Amen.

8

THE SIXTH BEATITUDE

'Blessed are those who hunger and thirst for righteousness, for they will be filled' (Matt. 5:6).

Jesus went up a mountain to a valley, into a field, and power went out of him as he preached to the great crowd: 'Blessed are those who hunger and thirst for righteousness, for they will be filled' (Matt. 5:6).

This text is relevant to what I am saying. Blessed are those who hunger for righteousness and endure work and poverty here, for this life is but a moment and will surely pass. They are blessed, though not most blessed. Blessed are those who hunger not to be deprived of God, albeit the wonder is that man can be without him without whom he cannot be. St Augustine says it is amazing that anyone should live apart from him, apart from whom he cannot live at all. They are blessed, and yet not most blessed. More blessed are those who so hunger that they cannot live without God; that is a fiery love which transforms their nature. As long as a man still finds anything impermanent in his desire or his hope or his love, he is not most blessed. He is blessed, but not most blessed. Blessed, supremely blessed, are those who are installed in the eternal now, transcending time and place and form and matter, unmoved by well-being or woe or wealth or want, for to the extent that things are motionless, they are like eternity.

The heaven adjoining the eternal now, in which the angels are, is motionless, immovable. But the heaven next to that, and between that and the heaven where the sun is, is set in motion by angelic force, revolving once in every hundred years. The heaven the sun is in, moved by angelic force, goes round once a year. The heaven the moon is in, again, is driven by angelic force and goes round once a month. The nearer to the eternal now, the more immovable they are, and the further off and more unlike the eternal now, the easier to move. The heaven of the sun and moon and stars is moved by the impulse of their angel, so that they are spinning in this temporal now. The eternal now gives them their motion, and it is so energetic that from the motion given by the eternal now, all things derive their life and being.

Now the lowest powers of the soul are nobler than the highest part of heaven, where it adjoins the angels and the eternal now. Moreover, all things get their life and being from the motion imparted by the eternal now; and if that is so noble, then what would you expect where the soul in her superior powers contacts the ground of God? Think how exalted that must be! So then, pursue this eternal now, reach this now and possess it. May we stand next to the eternal now, and so be in possession of it. So help us, O divine power.

One master says: 'Grace springs from the heart of the Father and flows into his Son, and in the oneness of the two of them it proceeds from the Wisdom of the Son into the Gift of the Holy Spirit, and in the Holy Spirit is sent into the soul. Grace is the face of God which is clearly stamped in the soul by the Spirit of God, giving the soul the form of God.' St Dionysius says: 'The angels are the divine mind.' Moreover, concerning those who live the angelic life here in the flesh, St Paul declares that into them there flows the mind of God, as it does into the angels. He also says that the intellectual light, namely God, has given likeness to the rational soul. St Paul says: 'He who unites himself with the Lord is one with him in spirit' (1 Cor. 6:17). So help us, God. Amen.

9

PEACE

'Jesus himself stood among them and said to them, "Peace be with you"' (Luke 24:36).

St John tells us in his Gospel that 'On the evening of that first day of the week, when the disciples were together, with the doors locked for fear of the Jews, Jesus came and stood among them and said, "Peace be with you!"' (John 20:19). 'Again Jesus said, "Peace be with you!"' (John 20:21). 'And with that he breathed on them and said, "Receive the Holy Spirit"' (John 20:22).

Now the evening never comes unless morning and midday have gone before. We say that the middle of the day is warmer than the evening. But insofar as evening takes in midday and stores up its heat, it is the warmer, especially when a whole bright day has gone before the evening. Again, late in the year, after the summer solstice, when the sun is drawing close to the earth, the evenings grow warm. But midday never comes till morning goes, nor evening until noon has passed away.

The moral of all this is that when the divine light breaks out in the soul, getting brighter and brighter until the perfect day, then morning does not vanish before noon nor noon before evening: they close up to one. So the evening is warm. There is perfect day in the soul when all the soul is full of divine light. But it is evening in the soul when the light of this world fades and the soul goes in to rest.

God said, 'Peace!' and, 'Peace!' again, and, 'Receive the Holy Spirit!' Jacob the patriarch came to a place, in the evening. He picked up some stones and, putting them underneath his head, he sank to rest. In his sleep he saw a ladder reaching up to heaven, with angels ascending and descending and God leaning down over the top of the ladder. This place had no name, which is as much as to say: the Godhead alone is the place of the soul, and is nameless. Concerning this, our doctors say: A thing which is another's place must be above it, as heaven is the place of all things and fire is the place of air and air the place of water and water, partially, the place of earth and earth is not a place. An angel is a heavenly place, and any angel who has got the least drop more of God than any other is the place, the habitation, of that other, the most exalted angel being the place, the room, the measure of the rest while he himself is without measure. But although he is without measure, nevertheless, God is his measure.

Jacob rested in the place which is nameless. By not naming it, it is named. On getting to this nameless place the soul will rest. Where all things are being God in God, there she will rest. The dwelling-place of the soul, which God is, is unnamed. I say, God is unspoken. But St Augustine says that God is not unspoken; were he unspoken, even that would be speech, and he is more silence than speech. One of our most ancient philosophers, who found the truth long, long before God's birth, before ever there was a Christian faith at all, said that to him it seemed that what he could manage to utter of things only conjured up within him something monstrous and unreal. Therefore he refused to speak at all. He would not even say, 'Give me some meat or give me a drink.' He declined to mention things because he could not say them as perfectly as when they sprang from their first cause. He chose rather to be dumb and to make known his wants by pointing with his finger. How much more does it become us to be absolutely mute concerning the One who is the origin of all things.

We say that God is a spirit. Not so. If God were really a spirit he would be spoken. According to St Gregory, we cannot rightly speak of God at all. Anything we say of him is bound to be a stammering. This place which is not named, in which all creatures thrive and bloom in orderly array, this habitat of all creatures, is born suddenly out of the ground of this orderly place, the seat of the soul proceeding out of this ground.

Jacob wanted to rest – notice, he wanted to rest. The rest of whoever rests in God is will-free. We say that will is without habit. Will is free. It takes nothing from matter. In this sense it is freer than intellect. Pouncing upon this, some rash people would put it above knowledge. That is not so. Intellect is also free, even though intellect does take from matter and from bodily things in the locality of the soul, for some of the soul-powers are linked with the five senses, for instance, with sight and hearing, which convey to them the things we know. A master says: 'God would never choose that eye or ear should sense what crowns the summit of the soul: none other than the nameless place, which is the place of all things.' It gives a fair reflection, and is useful in that way, but is marred by colour and by sound and corporal things. It is only by the senses that the soul is roused and the idea of wisdom naturally imprinted in her. Plato says, and with him St Augustine: 'The soul has all knowledge within, and all we can do from without is but an awakening of knowledge.'

Jacob rested in the evening. Let us always pray for the now; 'tis but a little thing we ask, just for one evening. May it be granted us. So help us, God. Amen.

EVERY GOOD GIFT

St James says in his epistle, 'Every good and perfect gift is from above, coming down from the Father of the heavenly lights' (Jas. 1:17).

Now for people who give themselves to God and diligently seek to do his will, whatever God may send will be the best. As God lives, you can be sure it is the very best, and there can be no better way. Some other way may seem better, yet is not so good for you. God wills this way and not that, therefore this way is bound to be the best. Whether it be sickness or poverty, hunger or thirst, what God gives or does not give, that is the very best for you. Yes, even though, sadly, you may be lacking in fervour for God or the interior life. Whatever you have or have not, accept it all to the glory of God, and then whatever he sends you will be for the best.

Perhaps you will say, 'How can I tell whether this is God's will or not?'

If it were not God's will, it would not be. You can have neither sickness nor anything else unless God wills it. And therefore, since you know it to be God's will, you ought to rejoice in it and be so contented that any pain loses its sting. Yes, even in extreme pain, it would be altogether wrong to feel the least affliction or distress. Accept it from

God as the best, since it is bound to be the best thing for you. It is of the essence of God to will what is best. Then let me will it too; nothing should please me more.

Suppose there were someone I tried hard to please, and suppose I knew for certain that this person liked me in a grey coat more than any other, then there is no doubt that that coat would please me too, and I would prefer it to any other, however nice. Given, then, my wish to please that person, I would do the things that I know please him both in word and action – and I would only do those things.

Well, then, judge for yourself how much you love. If you do indeed love God, you will like nothing better than whatever best enables him to work his will in you. No matter how great the apparent pain or deprivation, unless you take as much delight in it as in your ease and plenty, you are wrong.

One thing I often point out: it is a fact that every day we say in the Lord's Prayer, 'Lord, your will be done.' And yet when his will is done we grumble and are dissatisfied. Whatever God does, let us consider that to be the best, and like that best of all. Those who do take it as the best always stay calm. Sometimes you will say, 'Oh dear! It would be better if something else had happened.' Or, 'If that hadn't happened, things would have turned out better.' As long as you think like that, you will never be at peace. Accept it all for the best. That is the first thing our text teaches.

There is another meaning – note it carefully. James says 'every gift', that is, the very best and the very highest. These are innate gifts, and are in him who is the most innate of all. God gives nothing so gladly as great gifts. Once in this very place I said that God likes forgiving big sins more than small ones. The bigger they are, the gladder he is and the quicker to forgive them. It is the same with graces, gifts and virtues: the greater they are, the greater his pleasure in bestowing them, for generosity is his nature. The bigger the things and the better, the more

you will get. [The noblest creatures are the angels, who
are minds and nothing else; they do not have a physical
body, and they are infinitely more in number than all the
bodily things.]

I once laid it down that to be properly expressed a thing
must proceed from within, moved by its form: it must not
come in from outside, but go outside from within. It really
lives in the recesses of the soul. There all things are present to you, subjectively alive and active in their zenith, in
their prime. Why are you unaware of it? It is because you
are not at home.

The more noble a thing, the more prevalent it is. Feelings, I have in common with the beasts, and life in common with the trees. Being is even more innate in me, and
that I have in common with all creatures. Heaven exceeds
all neighbouring things, and it is nobler also. The nobler
the thing, the bigger it is and the more universal.

Love is as noble as it is universal. It does indeed seem
hard to follow our Lord's command and love our fellow
Christians as ourselves. The unenlightened say that we
ought to love them as they love themselves. Not so. We
ought to love them no more than our own selves, which is
not difficult. If you think about it, it is a reward more than
a command. The command seems hard but the reward
desirable. Whoever loves God as he ought and must
(whether he wishes to or not), and as all creatures love
him, will love his fellow Christian as himself, rejoicing in
his joys and hoping for his honour as much as for his own,
and treating the other like himself. In this way, he is
always happy, whatever his circumstances, just as though
he were in heaven, and moreover has more to enjoy than
his own blessings alone.

The plain truth is that it is wrong for you to regard your
honour as of more value than another's. Remember, if
you seek anything for yourself, you will never find God,
for you are not simply seeking God, you are seeking for
something with God. You are, as it were, making a candle

out of God with which to find something, and then, having found it, throwing the candle away. This is what will happen: anything that you find with God will be nothing, whatever it may be, whether profit or wages or the interior life or anything else: nothing is what you seek, and nothing you will find. All creatures are a mere nothing. I don't say they are small, but are something, I say they are absolutely nothing. A thing without being is not (or is nothing). Creatures have no real being, for their being consists of being in the presence of God. If God turned away for an instant, they would all perish. I have sometimes said, and it is true, that he who has got the whole world plus God has got no more than God by himself. Having all creatures without God is no more than having one fly without God; it is just the same, no more nor less.

This is a true saying: The man who gives a thousand marks of gold to establish convents or churches is doing a great deed. But the man who gives a thousand marks for nothing is doing far more. When God created all creatures, he could not move in them, they were so small and narrow. But he made the soul so like himself, so nearly his own peer, for the purpose of giving himself to her that she would not care in the least for anything else that he could give her. God must give me himself for my own as he is his own, or I shall get nothing, nor is anything else to my taste. Whoever receives him outright in this way must have renounced himself wholly and gone out of himself. All that he has he gets directly from God; it is his own just as much as it is God's, and our Lady's and all the inhabitants of heaven. All this is right and proper for him. Those who have renounced themselves and in this sense are dead to themselves receive the same, no less.

Thirdly, the term 'Father of the heavenly lights'. The word *father* implies a son. *Father* stands for abstract generation, and denotes the universal principle of life. The Father generates his Son in his eternal intellect. And just as he gives birth to his Son in his own nature, so he gives birth to the Son in the soul. He bears his Son in the soul as her own, and his existence depends on his bringing his Son to birth in the soul, whether he wishes to or not.

On one occasion I was asked what the Father is doing in heaven. I said that he is giving birth to his Son, an act he so delights in and which pleases him so much that he does nothing else but generate his Son, and these two are flowering with the Holy Spirit. When the Father gives birth to his Son in me, I am his Son and not another: we are another in manhood, true, but there I am the Son himself and no other. As sons we are lawful heirs. Anyone who knows the truth knows this very well. The word *father* connotes giving birth and having sons. We are sons in his Son, and we are the Son himself.

Now consider the words, 'is from above'. Referring to this, I said, 'Whoever wishes to receive from above must live in true humility below.' You can be sure that if he does not, he receives nothing and conceives nothing: not a single thing, however small. If your eye is on yourself or any thing or person, then you are not right under God, and you receive nothing. But being brought to this place, you receive everything at once and in perfection. It is God's nature to give, and his existence depends on his giving to us when we are in true humility. If we are not, then we get nothing: we do him violence and kill him. Or, if unable to do that, we do it to ourselves as far as it lies in us. If you would really give him everything, see to it that you put yourself under God in complete humility, raising up God in your heart and understanding.

The Father sent his Son into the world in the fullness of the soul's time, when she had finished with time. When the soul is free from time and place, the Father sends his Son into the soul. This is the explanation of the words, 'Every good and perfect gift is from above, coming down from the Father of the heavenly lights.' Let us be ready to receive these best gifts. So help us, God the Father of lights. Amen.

11

THE KINGDOM OF GOD IS NEAR

*'Even so, when you see these things happening, you know
that the kingdom of God is near' (Luke 21:31).*

Our Lord says, 'the kingdom of God is near'. Yes, the
kingdom of God is within us, and according to St Paul, our
salvation is nearer than we think. In what sense is the
kingdom of God near? Let us think about this carefully.
Suppose that I were the king without knowing it, then I
would be no king. But suppose I have a firm conviction
that I am the king, and everyone maintains this, and insists
upon it with me, and I know for certain that all the world
is of the same opinion, in that case I am king and all the
king's treasure is mine. Failing any one of these three
things, I cannot be the king.

In the same way, our happiness depends on our knowledge, our awareness of the sovereign good, which is God
himself. In my soul I have one power that is fully aware of
God. I am as certain as I live that nothing is as close to me
as God. God is nearer to me than I am to my own self; my
life depends upon God's being near me, present in me. He
is also present in a stone, or a log of wood, only they do
not know it. If the wood knew of God and realised his
nearness as the highest angel does, then the log would be
as blessed as the chief of all the angels. Man is more happy

70

than a log of wood in that he knows and is aware of God, and of how close at hand God is. The better he knows it the happier he is, and the worse he knows it the more unhappy he is. He is not happy because God is in him and so near to him, or because he has God, but because he is aware of God, of his nearness to him, because he is God-knowing and God-loving, and such a man knows that God's kingdom is at hand.

When I think about God's kingdom, I am often dumbfounded by its grandeur, for God's kingdom is God's self in all his fullness. God's kingdom is no little thing: if you put together all the worlds that God could possibly create, it would not make up his kingdom. No man dare counsel or instruct the soul in whom God's kingdom dawns, who is conscious of God's fullness. She is instructed by God and assured of life eternal. He who knows, who is aware, how near God's kingdom is can say with Jacob, 'Surely the Lord is in this place, and I was not aware of it' (Gen. 28:16).

God is just as near in his creatures. The wise man says, 'God has spread his nets and lines all over his creatures, and we can find and know him in any one of them if only we will look.'

A philosopher says, 'That man knows God aright who is equally aware of him in all things'; and, 'To serve God in fear is good; to serve him in love is better; but he who is apt to behold love in fear does best of all.' A life of rest and peace in God is good; a life of pain lived in patience is still better; but to have peace in a life of pain is best of all. One may go in the fields and say one's prayers and be conscious of God or go to church and be conscious of God. If we are more conscious of God when we are in a quiet place, that comes of our own imperfection and is not due to God, for God is the same in all things and all places and is just as ready to reveal himself as far as it lies in him to do so. The man who always finds God the same is the man who knows him aright.

St Bernard says, 'Why does my eye see sky, and not my foot? Because my eye is like the sky, more than my foot.' For my soul to see God, then, she must be heavenly. What makes the soul alive to God in her, and aware of how close he is to her? My answer: Heaven permits no alien intrusion. No mortal deficiency can penetrate within to do it outrage. And the soul who knows God is so firmly established in God that nothing can reach her, not hope nor fear nor joy nor grief nor good nor ill nor nothing that would bring her down to earth.

Heaven is at all points equidistant from the earth. And likewise the soul ought to be equally remote from every earthly thing and no nearer to one than to another, but the same in joy, in grief, in having and in wanting. Whatever it may be, she must be dead, dispassionate, superior to it. Heaven is clear and unsullied in its brightness, free from any taint of time and place. No physical thing finds room there. Though not itself in time, its revolution is incredibly swift. Its course is timeless, though from its course comes time. Nothing hinders the soul from knowing God so much as time and place. Time and place are fractions, God is an integer. So if the soul knows God at all she must know him above time and space, for God is neither this nor that as these manifold things are: God is one.

If the soul would see God she must not look at anything in time. While the soul has regard for time and place or any such idea she can never recognise God. Before the eye can see colour it has to be rid of all colour. Before the soul can see God it must have nothing in common with anything. The one who sees God knows that creatures are nothing. When you compare one with another, creatures look fair and are something, but compare them with God, and they are nothing.

Further, I declare that any soul who sees God must have forgotten herself and have lost her own self. While she sees and remembers herself she neither sees nor is conscious of God. But when for God's sake she loses herself and abandons all things, then she re-finds herself in God, for knowing God she knows herself and all things (which she had rid herself of) in God in perfection. Really to know the sovereign good and the eternal goodness, I must know them in the good itself, not in partial goodness. To know real being I must know it as subsisting in itself, that is, in God, not parcelled out in creatures.

In God alone rests the whole of divinity. The whole of manhood does not exist in one single man. But in God the soul finds perfect manhood and all things in their prime, for she knows them in their essential nature. Someone who lives in a richly furnished house must know far more about it than another person who, though full of information, has never been in it. And in the same way, I am as certain as I live, and as God lives, that the soul who knows God knows him above time and place. In this God-conscious state the soul perceives how near God's kingdom is, that is, God in all his fullness.

There is much discussion among doctors at the School about the possibility of the soul knowing God. God does not exact so much from man out of hardness, but out of his great kindness. He wants the soul to be more capacious, to be big enough to hold the largesse he is anxious to bestow.

Let no one think that it is difficult to arrive at this, however hard it may seem to start with, and indeed may actually be, to part from and die to all things. Having once got into it, no life is more easy, more delightful or more lovely. God is so very careful always to be with a man to guide him to himself in case that man takes the wrong way. No man ever wanted anything as much as God wants to make the soul aware of him. God is always ready, but we are so unready. God is near to us, but we are far from him. God is in, we are out; God is at home, we are strangers. The prophet says, 'God leads the just by a narrow path to the high road out into the open,' that is, to the true freedom of the spirit which has become one spirit with God. It is ours to follow, his to lead. We let him bring us to himself. So help us, God. Amen.

12

THE POOR IN SPIRIT

'Blessed are the poor in spirit, for theirs is the kingdom of heaven' (Matt. 5:3).

The Beatitude opened its mouth of wisdom and said, 'Blessed are the poor in spirit, for theirs is the kingdom of heaven.' Angels and saints and everything that has ever been born, must all keep silent when the eternal wisdom of the Father speaks; for the wisdom of the angels and all creatures is a mere nothing compared with the wisdom of God which is unfathomable. This wisdom has declared that the poor are blessed.

There are two kinds of poverty. One is outward poverty, and this is good and much to be commended in the one who makes a voluntary practice of it for the sake of our Lord Jesus Christ. But there is another poverty, an interior poverty, to which our Lord is referring when he says, 'Blessed are the poor in spirit' or 'poor of spirit'. And if you wish to understand my argument I urge you now to seek this poverty of spirit. For by the eternal truth I assure you that unless you are like this truth we speak of, it is not possible for you to follow me. Several people have asked me what poverty is. We will now try to give an answer.

Bishop Albertus says, 'By a poor man is meant one who

74

is not satisfied with anything God ever made,' and this is
well said. Better still, taking poverty in a higher sense, we
say that a poor man is one who wills nothing, knows nothing and has nothing. It is on these three points that I propose to speak.

emptiness
signlessness
wishlessness

In the first place, a poor man wills nothing. Some
people misunderstand the meaning of this – those, for
example, who win personal repute by penances and outward disciplines (God have mercy on them, they are
highly regarded, though they know so little of God's
truth!). To all outward appearances, they are holy, but
they are fools within and are ignorant of divine reality.
These people define a poor man as one who wills nothing,
explaining this to mean that he never follows his own will
at all, but is bent on carrying out the will of God. In this,
he is not bad. His intention is good, and we commend him
for it: God keep that man in his mercy. But in my opinion
such people are not poor men, nor are they the least like
them. They are much admired by those who know no better, but I maintain they are fools with no understanding of
God's truth. Perhaps heaven is theirs because they mean
well, but they have no concept of the poverty about which
we are talking.

If someone were to ask me, 'What then is a poor man
who wills nothing?' I should answer like this. As long as it
can be said of a man that it is in his will, that it is his will,
to do the will of God, that man has not the poverty that I
am speaking of, because he has a will to satisfy the will of
God, which is not as it should be. If he is genuinely poor, a
man is as free from his created will as he was when he was
not. I tell you by the eternal truth, as long as you possess
the will to do the will of God and have the least desire for
eternity and God, you are not really poor: the poor man
wills nothing, knows nothing, wants nothing.

While I was still in my first cause I had no God and I was
my own; I willed not, I wanted not, for I was conditionless
being, the knower of myself in divine truth. Then I wanted

myself and wanted nothing else; what I willed I was, and what I was I willed. I was free from God and all things. But when I escaped from my free will to take on my created nature, then I got me a God, for before creatures were, God was not God: he was that he was. When creatures became and started creaturehood, God was not God in himself, but he was God in creatures.

Now we contend that God as God is not the final goal of his creatures, nor is their final goal the very great riches which the least creature has in God. If a flea had intellect and could intellectually plumb the eternal abyss of God's being out of which it came, then, so we maintain, God and all God is could not fulfil and satisfy that flea. Therefore we pray that we may be rid of God and gain the truth and enjoy eternity, for the highest angel and the soul are all the same in that place where I was and willed that I was and was that I willed. And so a man may be poor of will, willing and desiring as little as he willed and wanted when he was not. And in this way a man who wills nothing is poor.

Secondly, a poor man is a man who knows nothing. We have sometimes laid it down that a man ought to live as though he did not live, whether for himself, or truth, or God. But now we declare that a person in this poverty has got all he was when he did not live in any way – not for himself, nor for truth, nor for God. He is so liberated, so free of any kind of knowledge, that no idea of God is alive in him. For when man stood in the eternal species God, nothing else lived in him. What lived there was himself. And so we say that this man is as free from his own knowledge as he was when he was not. He lets God work as God wills, while he himself remains as idle as when he came from God.

Now the question is: Where does happiness lie most of all? Some masters say it lies in love; others, that it lies in knowledge and in love, and these come nearer to the mark. But we contend that happiness lies neither in knowledge nor in love. In the soul there is one thing from which both knowledge and love flow, but which, unlike the faculties of the soul, itself neither knows nor loves. Whoever knows this, knows the seat of happiness. This has no before nor after, nor does it expect anything to come, for it can neither gain nor lose. It is lacking, in the sense that in itself it knows nothing about working. It just is itself, enjoying itself God-fashion. And in this sense I say man ought to be idle and free, entirely unknowing, unaware of what God is doing in him. That is the way to be poor.

According to the masters, God is being, intellectual being which knows all things. But I say, God is not being, nor yet intellect, he is not someone who knows this or that. God is free from all things and he is all things. Being poor in spirit means being poor of all particular knowledge, like one who does not know anything – not God, nor creatures nor himself. Here there is no question of a man desiring to know or recognise the way of God. This is how a man is poor in knowledge of himself.

Thirdly, the poor man has nothing. It has often been said that perfection means not having mortal, earthly things. Maybe this is true in one particular case, that is, when it is voluntary. But this is not the sense in which I mean it. I have already said that the poor man is not the man who wants to do the will of God, but the man who lives in such a way that he is free from his own will and from the will of God, even as he was free when he was not. This is the deepest kind of poverty. Second, we say that a poor man is a man who has no knowledge of God's work in him. To be as free of knowing and perceiving as God is of all things is the barest poverty. But the third poverty, the most stringent, is having nothing.

Here I would remind you that I have often said, and eminent authorities have also said, that if one would be a fitting place for God to work in one must be devoid of things and of activities, both inwardly and outwardly. Now we are saying something else. Granted that a man is bare of everything, of creatures, of himself, of God, yet if it is still in him to provide God with the room to work in, then we affirm that as long as this is the case, then the man is not poor with the strictest poverty. It is not God's purpose that man should possess the place in which God does his work. Poverty of spirit means freedom from God and all his works, so that if God chooses to work in the soul he must be his own workshop, as he likes to be. When he finds a man who is so poor, then God is his own patient and his own operating room, since God is in himself the operation. Here in this penury, man is obeying his eternal nature – that he has been and that he is now and that he shall be for ever.

There is the question of those words of St Paul, 'By the grace of God I am what I am' (1 Cor. 15:10). Here the argument soars above grace, above understanding and above desire. The answer is that St Paul's words are true. That grace was not in him; the grace of God worked in him, perfecting him to unity, and then the work of grace was done. Grace having done its work, Paul remained as he was. He was a man too poor to have or be a place for God to work in. To preserve a place is to preserve a distinction. The reason why I pray to God to rid me of God is because conditionless being is above God and above distinction. It was there that I was myself, there I willed myself and knew myself to make this man. And in this sense I am my own cause, both of my nature which is eternal and of my nature which is temporal. For this I am born, and as for my eternal birth – I can never die. In my eternal mode of birth I have always been, am now, and shall eternally remain. What I am in time will die and come to nothing, for it is of the day and passes with the day. In my birth all things were born, and I was the cause of my own self and all things. If I had willed it, I would never have been, nor would anything; and if I had not been, then God would not have been either. It is not necessary to understand this.

One learned doctor says that his breaking-through is nobler than his emanation, that is, his flowing out of God. When I flowed out of God, then all things said: 'There is a God.' Nevertheless, this cannot make me blessed, for in it I acknowledge that I am a creature. But in my breaking-through, then, standing passive in the will of God, free of the will of God and all his works and also of God himself, I transcend all creatures and am neither God nor creature: I am that I was and that I shall remain now and for ever. Then I receive an impulse which carries me above all angels. In this impulse I apprehend such surpassing riches that I am not content with God as being God, as being all his godly works, for in this breaking-through I find that God and I are both the same. Then I am what I was, I neither wax nor wane, for I am the motionless cause that is moving all things. Now God can find no place in man, for by his poverty man has got that which he has been eternally and will remain for ever. Here in the spirit God is one, that is the strictest poverty a man can know.

If anyone is unable to follow this discourse, he should not put his mind to it. While he is not like this truth he will not see my argument, for it is the naked truth straight from the heart of God. May we so live that we experience it eternally. So help us, God. Amen.

PART II

TRACTATES

1

THE BOOK OF COMFORT

'Praise be to the God and Father of our Lord Jesus Christ, the Father of compassion and the God of all comfort' (2 Cor. 1:3).

That great teacher St Paul says in his epistle, 'Praise be to the God and Father of our Lord Jesus Christ, the Father of compassion and the God of all comfort, who comforts us in all our troubles' (2 Cor. 1:3–4). Three kinds of trouble may fall on a man and plunge him into distress. First, harm to his external possessions; next, to his dearest friends; lastly, shame, hardship, physical pain and distress of mind to himself.

In the first place, we must bear in mind that the wise and wisdom, the true and truth, the good and goodness, the righteous and righteousness are closely related to each other. Goodness is not made nor created nor begotten: it is creative and gives birth to goodness. The good man, so far as he is good, is the unmade, uncreated but nevertheless the begotten child and son of goodness. Goodness reproduces itself and all it is in good things: in knowledge, love, energy. Goodness pours out of all of them into the good man, and the good man receives all his being, knowing, love and energy from the central depth of goodness, and from that alone. The good and goodness are no more than goodness by itself, except as unborn parent and born child of goodness. In the good there is only one being and one life. A good man gets all that belongs to him from the good and in the good. There he is and lives and dwells, and there he knows himself. He wills and works for everything he knows and loves. He works with goodness and in goodness, and the good does all its work with him and in him, as it is written. The Son said, 'It is the Father, living in me, who is doing his work. Believe me when I say that I am in the Father and the Father is in me' (John 14:10–11); his giving is my taking.

We must remember, further, that the Name or Word stands for nothing else, nothing more, nor less, than the good, pure and simple. But when we call him good we understand his goodness to be given him, infused and engendered by the unborn goodness. In the words of the Gospel: 'As the Father has life in himself, so he has granted the Son to have life in himself' (John 5:26). *In* himself, he says, not *from* himself, for the Father gave it to him.

Now all that I have said of the good and goodness applies equally to the true and truth, to the right (or just) and righteousness (or justice), to the wise and wisdom, to God's Son and to God the Father, to every God-begotten thing that has no father upon earth and in which there is no created thing: nothing that is not God, and in which there exists no form at all but that of God alone. St John says in his Gospel, 'to them gave he power to become the sons of God . . . which were born, not of blood, nor of the will of the flesh, nor of the will of man, but of God' (John 1:12–13, AV).

By 'blood' he means everything in man which is not subject to the human will. By 'the will of the flesh' he means everything in man which obeys his will, although perhaps with reluctance and inclined to physical desires, whatever is part of the body and the soul and is not confined to the soul alone. This accounts for the weakness and exhaustion of their powers. By 'the will of man' St John means the highest faculty of the soul. Its nature and energy, unmixed with flesh, resides in the pure nature of the soul, cut off from time and place and from everything that savours of time and place, from everything that has nothing in common with nothing. Here man is formed in the image of God. Here he is of the lineage of God, and God's family. Yet since these are not God himself, but are products of the soul and are in the soul, they have to lose their form and be transformed into God alone: born into God and out of God with only God for father. Then they are the Son indeed, God's only Son.

I am his Son because he gives birth to me in his nature and forms me in his image. Such a person is the Son of God, the good son of goodness, the right son of righteousness. As far as he is simply good, he is unborn parent, and as born Son he has the same nature as righteousness has, and is, and he is possessed of all the character of justice and truth. In all this teaching which is found in the holy gospel and confirmed in the natural light of the wise soul there is solace for every human sorrow.

St Augustine says, 'God is not far nor long. If you wish to find him without distance and length, commit yourself to God, for there a thousand years are as one day, today.' And I also say, in God there is no pain or sorrow or distress. And if you wish to be free from all adversity and pain, turn and cling to God and to God alone. Without doubt all your sufferings are because you have not turned to God and to God alone. If you were formed and born in righteousness alone, things could no more pain you than righteousness could, or God himself.

Solomon says, 'The righteous will not grieve for anything that may befall him.' He does not say the righteous man or the righteous angel, not this or that right thing, just 'righteous', being right. For the righteous man is a son with a father upon earth. He is a creature, who has been made or created, just as his father is a creature, made or created. Solomon says 'righteous', pure and simple, and that has no made or created father, for righteousness is the same as God. So pain and sorrow can no more molest him than they can God. Justice will not grieve him, for love and joy and bliss are justice, and if justice made the just sorrowful it would be causing sorrow to itself. Injustice and inequality cannot in any way grieve the just, for anything created is so far beneath him that it has no influence and makes no impression on the righteous, nor can it enter into him whose only father is God.

A man, then, ought to set to work and unform himself of himself and creatures, and know no father except God alone. Then nothing will be able to afflict or cast him down, neither God nor creatures, uncreated or created. Then his entire being, life, knowledge, love and wisdom will be from God and in God and God.

There is another thing which comforts us when troubles come. It is the certainty that the just and good man delights unspeakably, incomparably more in doing right than he or even the chief angel delights and rejoices in the management of his affairs or his life itself. The saints will gladly sacrifice their lives for right.

When difficulties come, if the good man stays calm and keeps his peace of mind, this only proves my point that the righteous man is proof against external events. But if anyone is put out by these misfortunes, if, while pretending to be righteous and fondly imagining himself to be so, a man is upset by such small things, then it stands to reason that God was just when he sent them. Since it is fair of God, he should not mind. In fact, he should rejoice in his sufferings much more than he does in his own life, or in the things other people find to rejoice in, for they do him more good than this world all told. For what use is the whole world to a man when he is no more?

The third important thing for us to understand is the elemental truth that the fount and living artery of universal good, essential truth and perfect consolation is God and God only. Everything that is not God has in itself a natural bitterness, discomfort and unhappiness. It does not make for the good which is of God and is the same as God, but lessens, dims and hides the sweetness, joy and comfort that God gives.

And further, I maintain that all sorrow comes from love of those things of which loss deprives me. If I mind the loss of outward things it is a certain sign that I am fond of outward things and really love sorrow and discomfort. Is it to be wondered at that I am unhappy when I like discomfort and unhappiness; when my heart seeks and my mind gives to creatures the good that is God's own? I turn towards creatures, from which there naturally comes all discomfort, and turn my back on the natural source of happiness and comfort. No wonder that I am gloomy and wretched! The fact is, it is quite impossible for God or anyone to bring true comfort to a man who looks for it in creatures. But the one who loves only God in creatures, and creatures in God only, that man finds real and true and equal comfort everywhere.

2

DETACHMENT

I have read many writings by heathen philosophers and sages, of the old covenant and the new, and have sought earnestly and with the greatest diligence to find the best and highest virtue. This is the virtue which will enable someone to knit himself most closely to God and in which he is most like his exemplar, as he was when he was in God, when there was no difference between himself and God, before God created creatures. And having studied all these Scriptures to the best of my ability, I find that this virtue is none other than absolute detachment from all creatures. Our Lord said to Martha, 'Only one thing is needed' (Luke 10:42), which is as good as saying that anyone who wishes to be serene and pure needs only one thing: detachment.

Our doctors sing love's praises, as did St Paul, who said, 'If I . . . have not love, I gain nothing' (1 Cor. 13:3). But I extol detachment above any love. First, because at best love constrains me to love God. Now it is far better for me to constrain God than for me to be constrained by God. My eternal happiness depends on God and me becoming one; but God is more inclined to adapt himself to me and can more easily communicate with me than I can with him. Detachment forces God to come to me. The reason why I say this is that everything likes to be in its own natural

88

state. God's own natural state is unity and purity, and these come from detachment. Hence God is bound to give himself to a heart that is detached.

Secondly, I rank detachment above love because love constrains me to suffer all things for God's sake, whereas detachment constrains me to receive nothing but God. Now it is far better to accept nothing but God than to suffer all things for God's sake. For in suffering one is concerned with creatures, from whom the suffering comes, but detachment is free from creatures. I can demonstrate that detachment accepts no one but God in this way: anything that is received must be received in something. But detachment is so nearly nothing that there is nothing rarefied enough to stay in this detachment, except God. He is so simple, so ethereal, that he can live in the solitary heart. Detachment, then, accepts God alone. Anything which is received is received and grasped by its receiver in accordance with the make-up of the receiver. And so anything conceived is known and understood according to the mind of him who understands, and not according to its own innate conceivability.

The masters praise humility more than most other virtues. But I rank detachment before any meekness, and for the following reasons. Meekness can be without detachment, but complete detachment is impossible without humility. Perfect humility lies in making the self nothing, but detachment approximates so closely to nothing that there remains no room for anything between zero and absolute detachment. Therefore, without humility you cannot have complete detachment. And two virtues are always better than one.

Another reason why I rank detachment higher than humility is this: humility means abasing the self before all creatures, and in that same abasement one goes out of oneself to creatures. But detachment stays in itself. Now no going out of oneself, however excellent, is better than staying still. As the prophet has it, 'All glorious is the princess within . . .' (Ps. 45:13). Perfect detachment pays no attention to creatures. It is without lowliness and loftiness. It has no interest in being below or above. It is intent on being master of itself, loving no one and hating no one, having neither this nor that, being neither like nor unlike any creature. The only thing it would like to be is the same. But it has no desire at all to be either this or that. He who is this or that is something; but detachment is absolutely nothing. It leaves things unmolested.

At this point someone may object: 'But surely in our Lady all the virtues flourished in perfection, and among them absolute detachment. Now granting that detachment is better than humility, why did our Lady glory in her lowliness instead of her detachment, and say, "He has been mindful of the humble state of his servant" (Luke 1:48)?'

My answer is that in God there is both detachment and humility – so far as virtues can be attributed to God. When God was made man, it was his loving meekness that made him stoop to enter human nature while it remained motionless within itself. And it was in meekness that he created the heavens and the earth, as I shall show you later. And when our Lord chose to be made man, he persisted in his motionless detachment. That was how our Lady knew that he expected her to be the same, even though for the time being he paid particular attention to her lowliness and not to her detachment. So, while not moving from her detachment, she nevertheless gloried in her lowliness and not in her detachment. Had she but once remembered her detachment enough to say, 'He regarded my detachment,' her detachment would have been disturbed and would not have been absolute and perfect, since a going out had taken place. Any event, however insignificant, will always cause some troubling of detachment. And there you have the explanation of our Lady's glorying in her lowliness instead of her detachment.

The prophet said, 'I will listen to what God the Lord will say' (Ps. 85:8), as though to say, if God would confer

with me, then he must come in, for I will not go out. It is
Boethius who exclaims, 'You men, why do you look without for that which is within you?'

I prize detachment more than mercy, too, for mercy
means nothing else but a man's going out of himself
because his heart is wrung and goes out to his fellow men
in their need. Detachment is free from this; it stays within
itself, allowing nothing to disturb it. In short, when I
reflect on all the virtues, I find not one so wholly free from
fault, so able to unite me to God, as detachment.

It was Avicenna the philosopher who said, 'The mind
detached is of such nobility that what it sees is true, what it
desires comes about, and its wishes must be obeyed.' For
you must know that when the free mind is quite detached
it constrains God to itself. If it could remain formless and
free from outside events, it would take on the nature of
God. But God grants this to no one apart from himself; so
God can do no more for the solitary soul than make it a
present of himself. The man who is in absolute detachment is carried away into eternity where nothing temporal
affects him nor is he in the least aware of any mortal thing.
The world is well and truly dead to him, for he has no taste
for any earthly thing. St Paul meant this when he declared,
'For to me, to live is Christ and to die is gain' (Phil. 1:21).

Perhaps you will say, 'What is detachment, then, that it
should be so noble in itself?'

True detachment means a mind as little moved by what
happens, by joy and sorrow, honour and disgrace, as a
broad mountain by a gentle breeze. Such motionless
detachment makes a man superlatively godlike. For God
is God because of his motionless detachment; he gets his
purity and his simplicity and his unchangeableness from
his detachment. If, then, a man is going to be like God, so
far as any creature can resemble God, it will be by detachment. This leads to purity, and from purity to simplicity,
and from simplicity to immovability. These three consti-
tute the likeness between man and God, and this likeness

is of grace, for it is grace which draws a man away from mortal things and purges him from corruptible things. I would have you know that to be empty of creatures is to be full of God, and to be full of creatures is to be empty of God.

Now it must be remembered that God has always existed in this unchanging detachment, and does so still. When God created the heavens and the earth he might not have been making anything at all for all that it affected his detachment. Indeed, I say more than this: prayers and good works performed by a man in time no more affect the divine detachment than if no prayers or virtuous works had taken place in time. Nor is God any more kindly disposed towards such a man than if his prayers and deeds had all been left undone. Further, I declare that when the Son in his Godhead was pleased to be made man and lived on earth and suffered martyrdom, God's motionless detachment was no more disturbed than if he had never been made man.

Maybe you will say, 'I gather then that prayers and good deeds are useless since God takes too little interest in them to be affected by them. And yet it is said that God likes to be prayed to on all occasions.'

Now mark this, and if possible understand it. In his first eternal glance (if a first glance may be assumed), God saw all things as they would happen, and in that same glance he saw both when and how he would make creatures. He saw the humblest prayer that would be offered, the least good deed that anyone would do, and, moreover, he saw which prayers and worship he would hear. He saw that tomorrow you will call upon him sincerely, desperately pleading with him, and he saw that, not for the first time, he would grant your request: he has granted it already in his eternity before you ever became man. Suppose your prayer is foolish or insincere, God will not say no to you tomorrow – he has already said no in his eternity. Thus God, who has seen everything in that first eternal glance, in no way acts from any cause at all, for everything is a foregone conclusion.

But though God always remains in motionless detachment, yet men's prayers and good works are not all in vain, for the man who does well is rewarded well. As Philippus says, 'The creator God holds all things in the course and order he gave them from the beginning.' With him nothing is past and nothing is future, and he loves all his saints just as he saw and loved them before ever the world became. Yet when the things which he contemplated in eternity come to pass in time, then people think that God has changed his mind. But whether he is angry or gracious, it is we who change and he who remains the same, just as the sunshine hurts weak eyes and helps strong eyes while the light itself remains unchanged. God does not see in time, nor is his outlook subject to alteration.

Isodorus argues along these lines in his book on the Arch-Good. He says that people are always asking what God did before he created the heavens and the earth, and that they want to know where God's new decision to make creatures came from. His answer is that God did not make a new decision at all, for even though creatures did not exist as they now do, yet they existed from eternity in God and in his mind. God did not make the heavens and the earth by saying, as man would say, 'Let them be!' but creatures are all spoken in his eternal Word. 'Moses said to God, "Suppose . . . the Israelites . . . ask me, 'What is his name?' Then what shall I tell them?" God said to Moses, "I AM WHO I AM . . . I AM has sent you"' (Exod. 3:13–14). In other words, 'He who is unchanging in himself is the one who has sent me.'

Here someone may object, 'But was Christ in motionless detachment when he cried, "My soul is overwhelmed with sorrow to the point of death" (Matt. 26:38)? Or Mary when she stood beneath his cross? A great deal is said about her grief. How is all this compatible with motionless detachment?'

You should know that according to philosophers in every person there are two people. First there is the outward person which is the objective nature served by the five senses, though energised by the power of the soul. Secondly, there is the inner person, the subjective nature. Now the godly-minded man employs the powers of his soul in his outward person no more than his five senses really need it; and his interior person only has recourse to the five senses insofar as it is the guide and keeper of these five senses and can stop them being put to bestial uses as they so often are by those who live according to the baser appetites, like the mindless animals and some people who deserve the name of beast rather than of man. When the soul has any surplus energy beyond that expended on the five senses, she bestows it upon her inner person. If her inner self is set upon some very high endeavour, she will call in all the powers she has loaned to the five senses. Then that man is said to be senseless and rapt away, his object being either some unintelligible form or some formless intelligible.

Remember, God requires every spiritual man to love him with all the powers of his soul. 'Love the Lord your God with all your heart' (Deut. 6:5), he says. Some squander all their soul's powers on their outward self. These are the people whose thoughts and feelings hinge on the things of this world, and are quite unaware of an inner person. And just as the good man will now and then deprive his outward self of all the powers of the soul whenever he is embarking on some high adventure, so the bestial man will rob his inner self of all its soul-powers to expend them on his outer self.

The outward person is able to be active and leave the inward person entirely passive and unmoved. Now in Christ too, and also in our Lady, there existed an outward and an inward person, and what Christ and our Lady said about outward things was prompted by their outward self while the inner self remained in motionless detachment.

That was the case when Christ said, 'My soul is overwhelmed with sorrow to the point of death' (Matt. 26:38). And despite her grief and the various things she said, in her inner self our Lady remained in motionless detachment. Take an illustration. The door goes to and fro upon its hinges. Now the door is like the outward person and the hinge is like the inner person. As it shuts and opens the door swings to and fro while the hinge remains unmoved in the same place without undergoing any change. And that is how it is here.

What then, I ask, is the object of absolute detachment? And I answer that the object of absolute detachment is neither this nor that. It is absolutely nothing, for it is the culminating point where God can do precisely as he wills. God cannot have his way in every heart, for though God is almighty, he can still only work where he finds readiness or makes it. I add, 'or makes it', because of St Paul, in whom God found no readiness but whom he made ready by an infusion of his grace. Therefore I affirm that God works according to the aptitude he finds. He works differently in man and in a stone. I can illustrate this with an analogy taken from nature. If you heat a baker's oven and put different kinds of dough in it, some made of barley, some of oats, some of wheat and some of rye, then even though the heat is the same throughout the oven, its effect is not the same – one dough yields a fine bread; another, one more coarse, and a third a coarser still. The heat is not to blame: it is the material which differs. Nor does God affect every heart in the same way, but his work varies according to the readiness and the capacity he finds. In any heart containing this or that there is something to hinder God's highest operation. For a heart to be perfectly ready it has to be perfectly empty. In this condition it has attained its maximum capacity. To take another common illustration, suppose I want to write on a piece of white card, then anything already written there, however excellent it may be, will interfere and hinder me from writing.

Before I can write I must erase whatever is already on the card. It is best of all when there is nothing there at all. And so for God to write his very best within my heart everything dubbed this or that must be ousted from my heart, leaving it quite without attachment. God is free to work his sovereign will when the object of this solitary heart is neither this nor that.

Then, again, I ask: 'What is the prayer of the solitary heart?' My answer is that detachment and emptiness cannot pray at all, for whoever prays desires something from God: something to be added to him or something to be taken from him. But the heart that is detached has no desire for anything, nor has it anything to be delivered from. So it has no prayers at all; its only prayer consists in being one with God. This is what St Dionysius is referring to when he comments on St Paul's words, 'In a race all the runners run, but only one gets the prize' (1 Cor. 9:24). All the powers of the soul are competing for the crown which falls to the essence alone. According to Dionysius, this running is none other than the flight from creation to union with uncreated nature. Gaining this, the soul loses her name; God absorbs her in himself so that as herself she comes to nothing, just as the sunlight swallows up the dawn and reduces it to nothing. Only absolute detachment brings the soul to this place.

St Augustine's words are relevant here: 'The soul has a private door into divine nature at the point where for her things all come to nothing.' This door on earth is none other than absolute detachment. At the height of her detachment the soul is ignorant with knowing, loveless with loving, dark with enlightenment.

Here, too, we might cite a master's words, 'Blessed are the spiritual poor who have abandoned unto God all things as he possessed them when we existed not.' Only a heart entirely without attachment can do this.

That God would sooner be in a solitary heart than any other, I maintain for the following reasons. I start with your question, 'What does God seek in all things?' and answer in his words out of the Book of Wisdom, 'In all things I seek rest.' Now perfect rest is found only in a heart that is detached. Therefore, God is happier there than in any other thing or virtue. The more we are disposed to receive the inflowing God, the more happy we shall be; perfect receptivity gives perfect felicity. Now one makes oneself receptive to the influence of God only by dint of uniformity with God; as a man's uniformity with God, so is his sense of the inflowing of God. Uniformity comes from subjection to God, and the more one is subject to creatures the less one is at one with God. But the heart which is quite detached and empty of creatures, utterly subject to God and at one with him in the highest degree, is wholly open to his divine inflowing. Hence St Paul's exhortation to 'Clothe yourselves with the Lord Jesus Christ' (Rom. 13:14), that is, uniformity with Christ. For when Christ was made man it was not a certain man that he assumed, he assumed human nature. If you go out of all things, then there remains only what Christ put on, and you have put on Christ.

Whoever is determined to know the excellence and use of absolute detachment, let him lay to heart Christ's words to his disciples on the subject of his manhood, 'It is for your good that I am going away. Unless I go away, the Counsellor will not come to you' (John 16:7), as though to say, 'You have too much love for my visible form for the perfect love of the Holy Spirit to be yours.' Therefore discard the form and unite with the formless essence, for God's spiritual comfort is intangible and is only offered to those who despise all mortal consolations.

Listen, good people: no one is happier than the one who stands in utter detachment. Every temporal, carnal pleasure brings some spiritual mischief in its train, for the flesh lusts after things that run counter to the spirit and the spirit lusts for things that are repugnant to the flesh. The one who sows the tares of love in the flesh reaps death, but the one who sows good love-seed in the spirit reaps eternal life from the spirit. The more man flees from creatures, the faster his Creator hastens to him. Think about it, all you thoughtful souls! If even the love which it is given us to feel for the bodily form of Christ can keep us from receiving the Holy Spirit, then how much more must the inordinate love of physical pleasures keep us from getting to God? Detachment is the best of all, for it cleanses the soul, clarifies the mind, kindles the heart and wakens the spirit. It quickens desire and enhances virtue, giving an awareness of God. It separates the soul from physical things and makes her one with God; for love apart from God is as water in the fire, but love in union is like the honeycomb in honey.

Listen, all rational souls! The swiftest steed to bear you to your goal is suffering. Only those who stand with Christ in depths of bitterness will ever taste eternal bliss. Nothing is more bitter than suffering, nothing so honey-sweet as to have suffered.

The most sure foundation for this perfection is humility. The one who creeps in deepest depths here will soar in spirit to the highest height of Deity; for joy brings sorrow and sorrow brings joy. Men's ways are many: one man lives in one way, another in a different way.

If you wish to attain to the highest life while living here in time, then listen to the following few words, the summary of a philosophy culled from all the Scriptures.

Keep yourself detached from all mankind; keep yourself devoid of all incoming images; emancipate yourself from everything which entails addition, attachment or encumbrance, and focus your mind at all times on the saving contemplation of God. Carry him within your heart as the fixed object from which your eyes never waver. Subordinate to this any other discipline, fasts, vigils, prayers, or whatever it may be, only engaging in them to the extent that they further your purpose. So you will win the goal of all perfection.

Here someone may object, 'But who can persist in unwavering contemplation of the divine object?'

I answer, no one living here in time. I have told you this merely so that you may know the highest, that on which your aspirations and desires should be set. But when this vision is withheld from you, you, being a good man, will think you have been robbed of your eternal bliss. Then you must return at once, that it may come to you again. Moreover, as far as is possible, you need to keep strict watch upon your thoughts at all times, letting their goal and refuge be this divine contemplation. Lord God, glory be to you eternally. Amen.

3

THE WAY

'I am the way and the truth and the life' (John 14:6), says our Lord Jesus Christ.

Note especially the words, 'I am the way.' We understand Christ to be the way in two senses: according to his manhood, and according to his Godhead.

His manhood was the way of our own manhood. This we have to follow – both the counsel of perfection as a whole and also in its parts. If just one part of our body leaves the way of his example, we are thereby deformed. St Paul declares that we ought to live in such a way that God may find in us the perfect reflection of all his divine works, that is, we must copy the model he has set before us. That is true spiritual life.

But this is greatly hampered by numerous defects, and especially numerous interior shortcomings due to the disorder of the soul's powers. The joy of the soul should be so set upon its own work that no created things can gladden her, but only the fact that her conscience is clear. As Christ said to his disciples, 'Do not rejoice that the spirits submit to you, but rejoice that your names are written in heaven' (Luke 10:20). And the soul's fear should be so well controlled that she is afraid of nothing under God. She has no fear for her person or her possessions, and fears nothing that may be inflicted upon her, whether by God or man. And similarly with the other powers, desire and thought. In short, the entire soul has to be gathered up into the indivisible simplicity of her will, and her will must fly towards the highest good and fasten itself to it. St Paul says, 'He who unites himself with the Lord is one with him in spirit' (1 Cor. 6:17).

See how rich the spirit is that has grown in this way into one spirit with God! No things can enrich it, though it rules over them all. For things are determined by this world, whereas the soul's riches consist in its dwelling in a nature superior to physical necessity. The man who has nothing and needs nothing is richer than the man who possesses all things with necessity. St Paul says: 'Our competence comes from God. He has made us competent as ministers of a new covenant (2 Cor. 3:5–6).

Nor do the virtues enrich the spirit. Doctors declare that, properly speaking, it is not the virtues which enrich the spirit, but the fruit of the virtues. The soul has virtues of necessity. But since virtues are a necessity, the spirit is of necessity not enriched by them. The utmost a spirit can attain to in this body is to dwell in a condition beyond the necessity of virtues, where goodness as a whole comes naturally to it, so that not only is it possessed of virtues but virtue is part and parcel of it. It is virtuous not of necessity but because its nature is innately good. At this point, the soul has traversed and transcended all necessity for virtues: they are now intrinsic to her. Now she has reached the goal to which the virtues merely pointed her, that is, the filling of the Holy Spirit. This is the fruit of virtue; this alone serves to enrich the spirit. Concerning this, St Paul says: 'Put on the new self, created to be like God' (Eph. 4:24), who was in this way our way.

The other way, the second of the two ways, is the way of Christ's Godhead.

What way has the Godhead, and where can it go since it is in all places; and how does it go since it has no feet nor any bodily thing?

The way of the Godhead is the unity in which the three Persons run together into one essence. The going of the Persons consists in their mutual knowing and loving, each knowing and loving itself in the others. In this way the Persons walk together in unity.

The feet with which the Godhead enters the Persons, and the Persons the essence, are as follows: one foot of the Godhead is foreknowledge of all things; the other, pleasure in the things eternally foreseen, for God eternally enjoys the contingency of things. This refers to the eternal image. God enjoys only good in all things: the image of all things which is true God.

It may be asked: What pleasure does God enjoy?

All things must please him, for the one who saw was God and what he saw was also God. In their eternal image which is God himself, God saw himself and saw things as a whole. God enjoyed himself, God being in himself the one who is unique. The soul sees that her indivisible archetype lies in God, and it has never come out of him.

What does leave God is the soul's multiform image, and the consummation of her spirit lies in the restoration of the soul's created something here in time to the nothingness of its eternal prototype. God is the origin of the spirit, and the spirit never rests till it returns into its origin, to its eternal prototype. In essence this prototype is God. Therefore it always eludes the spirit, which is never quite able to apprehend it. Yet the spirit senses how it has been eternally in God without itself, and the most supreme bliss the spirit knows is to sink back into its origin, to its eternal image, in which, as self, it is lost altogether. But the spirit loses its uses, not its essence. The essence of the Godhead seeks the spirit out of itself into itself, making it as itself, so that now there seems only one essence. It is as though I were to take a serpent's blood – which is very red – and pour it into a transparent glass; the glass would lose its appearance, but not its substance. So in this union the divine light illuminates and outshines the spirit, which shines as one light with it. The spirit loses its appearance, but not its substance, for God has brought the spirit out and united it with himself. Nevertheless, in this union the spirit can never plumb the depths of the Godhead, as St Paul discovered when, caught up to the third heaven, he saw things not permissible, indeed, not possible to speak about, and cried out: 'Oh, the depths of the riches of the wisdom and knowledge of God! How unsearchable his judgments, and his paths beyond tracing out!' (Rom. 11:33).

God's riches consist in having nothing and being nothing that can be clothed in words. His wisdom consists in the well-ordering of things. God's knowledge is his conception of himself in his heavenly light. Concerning this, St Dionysius says, 'The light God dwells in is his own nature which is known to none besides himself.' This is the highway of the Godhead which no creature has ever trod. God spoke of this through his prophet: 'As the heavens are higher than the earth, so are my ways higher than your ways' (Isa. 55:9). St Augustine says that there is nothing more difficult and more exacting but at the same time more useful and salutary to the soul than excursions in the science of the holy Trinity and unity.

Therefore pay careful attention to the meaning of the Persons and the essence.

What is a Person in the Trinity?

A Person preserves its own rational individuality separate from any other distinct Person. One Person is not another. The work of the Persons consists in the genesis and output of things. Genesis belongs to the Father alone; outputting of things to the Trinity jointly.

What is the essence of the three Persons in the Trinity?

Indivisible, it contains all things without division, while of itself as essence it neither generates nor produces things. This is done by the three Persons who activate the essence, or it could do nothing. Nevertheless, the Persons do not act as three; they work as one God.

What is the potentiality of the essence?

The potentiality of the essence lies in its not being a rational Person; in persisting in its essential unity. But it does not differ from the Persons; this same essence is the essential nature of the Persons and the being of all things. It is the existence of all existing things, the life of all living things, the light of lights and nature of natures: all this it is in its unity. Not so with the Persons: they are not the personality of things as essence is the essence of all things. The Father is not able to be anybody's person but his own. He gave birth to another Person out of his Person, not out of his essence: with his nature in his nature. That the Father was able to produce a Son so superbly, so consummately his like, a God as perfect as himself, is due to his essential nature.

When he gives birth to the Son, the Father gives him a Person other than his own Person, but not another nature nor another essence. It follows that the essence is revealed in the movement of the Persons. The Persons are able to reveal the essence which cannot of itself reveal itself, since of itself, as essence, it neither begets nor bears. This impotence of the essence is its chief potentiality; nevertheless it is revealed to itself.

The Persons know and comprehend the essence equally. The essence bears the same relation to all the Persons. Now, it is a point of discussion among theologians whether or not the personality has basic knowledge and comprehension of the essence, since the essence is comprehended only by the essence.

The Persons have basic knowledge and comprehension of the essence because the essence is the Persons' own essential nature. Moreover, the essence is only comprehended wholly by the three Persons, whose nature it is. The Persons comprehend the essence wholly since they are God in Person because of their comprehension of his essence which is their own essential nature. And so far as the soul comprehends this essence, she too is divine, though what she comprehends of it is no bigger than a drop compared with all the boundless ocean. Still it is wholly God. The surplus good which is always baffling her apprehension is the shadowy abyss in which, losing herself, she sinks eternally.

It may be questioned, 'Why is there not one Person, as there is one essence?'

My answer is that existing things do not exist from themselves, but in eternity they are descended from an origin which is the origin of its own self, and in time they have been created out of nothing by the blessed Trinity. Their eternal origin is the Father, and the universal image in him is the Son. The love for this same image is the Holy Spirit. If this archetype of all things had not always been in the Father, the Father could never have wrought anything at all, that is, in his modeless essence.

There must be more than one Person, for it was in the eternal procession of (that is, in the birth of) the Son that things as a whole flowed from the Father and not from themselves. This eternal procession is the cause of things on their eternal side, but in time they were created from nothing, and in this sense they are creatures. In the eternal procession in which they flowed out from themselves, they are God in God. For as St Dionysius says, the Prime Cause generates all things in the likeness of itself.

Now notice the difference between this emanation in eternity and in time. What is the temporal emanation? It is the expression of his love of clear discrimination. So we come out into time by the force of his love. The eternal procession is the revelation of himself to himself, the knower being that which is known. This is the eternal flow, no drop of which ever fell into any created intelligence; it is the Son from the Father. In the temporal emanation things flowed out in finite form. In the eternal emanation they remain infinite, the flow goes flowing on in itself. As St Dionysius has it, 'God is a fountain flowing into itself.' The Father is the origin of his Son, in his

eternal child-bearing; the Father and Son originate their
Spirit, in the eternal out-pouring.

'But,' someone may question, 'how about the Father-
nature? Is it the cause of the essence, or is the essence the
cause of the fatherhood?'

What follows needs clear thinking. Essence as essence
neither gives nor takes. Now if the essence were the origin
of the Father, then the essence, being parent, would not
be essence, it would be the Person. But it is not; for
essence in its unity is not a Person. Again, if paternity
were the origin of the essence, the cause of this would be
the paternal Person. But this is not the case either. The
Father in Person is a cause, but not of essence; for paternity and essence have the same characteristic. That is why,
in his fatherhood, he is the omnipotent cause. The essence
cannot be apart from the Person, nor can the Person be
apart from nature, as you can see. For nothing that exists
can be without its nature, since it cannot take leave of
itself; it must be what it is. Now the Father is a Person,
and he cannot be a Person without a nature, nor can his
nature be without a Person. Given his nature, there must
be someone whose nature it is. Note, then, that the
essence cannot exist without distinction and hypostasis,
that is, personal existence. And the Person and hypostasis
cannot be without their nature, that is, their essence.

In this way it is demonstrated that the essence is not the
cause of the fatherhood, nor the fatherhood the cause of
the essence, for neither can be without the other. The Son
cannot be without the Father, nor the Father without the
Son, nor the two without the Holy Spirit, although they
have three properties to distinguish them apart. Not so
with fatherhood and essence. Neither of these can be without the other. For although essence is not the Person, nor
the Person essence, yet paternity and essence have the
same nature, so that neither can be said to be the origin of
the other. For it is with one and the same nature that the
Father originates his Son, and these two originate their

Spirit which is of one nature with them both.

All hail to the exalted spirit that is received into this full, this naked truth and knowledge which is unknown to those who are not naked of themselves. For the soul to be naked, she must turn away from all the images and forms spread out before her and stop at none of them, for the divine nature has no form or appearance that she can understand. Being turned away from these towards what transcends them – divorced, that is, from images and forms – the soul receives the likeness of the formless nature of God, whose real form has never been revealed to any creature. This is the secret door into the divine nature, which the soul has in the image. For when the soul has nothing to hinder her, she is ready to pass into the image of God to which no one can attain unless he is stripped of spiritual matter. Alas, how they obstruct this secret passage, those who so lightly stop in temporal things! And here I also acknowledge my wretchedness. This is what St Dionysius was referring to when he exhorted his disciples with the words, 'If you wish to know the hidden mystery of God, transcend whatever hinders your pure perception.'

When her pure intellect is illumined with divine light the naked soul sees God, and then she knows herself. And when she sees how suited she is for him, how she is his and how they are both one, then, the burden of the body permitting, she remains like this always.

Job speaks of the lofty intuition that the soul has of the hidden mystery of God when he says: 'In the horror of a vision by night he comes and whispers in the ears of men' (Job 33:15–16). What does Job mean by the horror? He is expressing his solicitude for this perception of which we are speaking. The nocturnal vision is the revelation of the hidden truth. And the whispering is the flowing union in which knower and known are one.

Many people find this book difficult and obscure. I plead with you not to publish it, for God's sake, for it was forbidden to me to do so. If anyone should condemn it, that is the fault of his blindness, for it is the absolute truth. But if there are any things in it that could have been put in a better way, do not wilfully misunderstand them, for words fail in speaking of the divine nature. Its meaning is clear in the truth which is with Christ and in Christ. Therefore may he be blessed and praised for ever. Amen.

4

COMMENTARY ON ST JOHN'S GOSPEL

'In the beginning was the Word, and the Word was with God, and the Word was God' (John 1:1).

The profound Gospel of St John begins, 'In the beginning was the Word, and the Word was with God, and the Word was God.' Anyone who wishes to grasp the interpretation of these difficult writings of St John, which with God's help I will unfold, must turn his mind from created things and from his own understanding, so that, illumined by God's spirit, he may understand the meaning I give to these dark sayings.

To start with, I understand from John's words, 'in the beginning', a beginning without beginning. In God's name I continue. In the beginning was the Word. That is, at the source of the radiant light that gives form to rational creatures, and in the origin of its radiance, the Word existed as the perfect Word, perfect in its wordless potentiality. And this wordless word was with God. This hints at a distinction: the word being *with* God.

Now bring your best intelligence to bear on this. When the bound word of the Persons' unity remained unuttered by the omnipotent intellect, then the Word, suspended in its divine origin, transcended all words and names. When it was with God in the providential light dawning devoid of the created universe, then God was revealed to the world. Therefore I, Meister Eckhart, affirm this: as soon as God was, he created the world, the world being with God and distinct in name. Whereas God in his motionless power was free from God and every name, God was the unspoken word in the bottomless abyss of his divine nature in which the Word as such never thoroughly understood itself. A thing that understands itself grows and fades in the act of understanding, but this word does not grow or fade. It is unchanging in itself, so it has never understood itself in itself, even though it is the intellect of the Father.

It was in the beginning of the new procession of the Son that the Son proceeded out into the time of natural images, united with the word that always abides in the paternal source. This same Word wrought its entire work of nature in the form of a person, humanly, and the bound Word itself energises in the Father in his characteristic nature, this same word being eternally immanent by nature. And since this is the nature of the Word, it is permissible to say, 'In the beginning was the Word.'

I will now apply the interpretation to the human soul. If anyone cannot understand it, he should go to the truth for enlightenment.

In the beginning of the divine nature the soul is seeking herself above the points of time. Cast into the nothingness of the abyss of the divine nature, her receptivity all gone, her portion in her happiness is the perfect naught that distinguishes her from other creatures. As our Lord says, 'Be perfect, therefore, as your heavenly Father is perfect' (Matt. 5:48). But if the soul could know God with his own special nature, she would be loving something above God. Accordingly, I say that this word existing in the essential activity of the divine nature is the soul wholly deprived of receptivity, for with this she would be loving herself and all she is with a personal nature. So she may rightly affirm herself to be the work of God in the beginning where, although she is formless, she is expressing form. But the form she gets from God is gained by the sealing in the soul of God's own nature. In the beginning of her nothingness was the word, and the word was with God as Son, and the Word was God.

John goes on to say, 'He was with God in the beginning' (John 1:2). Notice, I have just said, 'In the beginning was the Word.' Now I say, 'He was with God in the beginning.' From these cryptic statements it appears that the Word was with God in the beginning. Now I suggest an obvious rational meaning. 'He was with God in the beginning': in the source of paternity. This source is the source of the entire Godhead of the Father, personal and essential, of Son and Spirit.

St John says, 'He was with God in the beginning.' Since in the Father there is an outpouring of his causeless divinity into the Word of his Son, this must occur in the paternal mind when, looking upon himself in the light of his abiding intellect, he perceives himself in the answering reflection in his divine essence; or, in other words, the conception of the Word is God.

Moreover, by this reflection of his divine nature, the intellect of the Father fashions or utters itself in imitation of his nature. So the Word is the Son, and it is in the divine substance, that is, in the intellectual reflection of the Father, that this birth of the proceeding Word occurs. Thus it is one in essence and distinct in Person. Hence we may say: 'He was with God in the beginning.' And because introspection and reflection of the divine nature are involved as it continuously thinks of itself, this birth is eternal. For if this reflection were once to stop, if a mental holiday, if inactivity, should once intervene, there would remain one God without the distinction of Persons. Thus the Word of the Father exists eternally in its parental origin. By this means it is always being conceived and being born and reborn. The same Word was in the father-principle with God as a distinct Person.

Next come the words, 'Through him all things were made; without him nothing was made that has been made' (John 1:3). Examine this carefully. Granting that all things were made by him and that nothing was made without him, then someone may ask me, 'Can God do anything without me seeing that through him all things were made and without him nothing was made that was made?' I answer, 'No.' God made all things with me standing in the groundless ground of God; God made all things through me while I stood idle in him. While the Father was performing this act that was so special to his nature, I was standing right in the gate through which all things return perfectly freely to their supreme happiness. As our Lord said, 'Father . . . Now this is eternal life: that they may know you, the only true God, and Jesus Christ' (John 17:1, 3). If eternal life is anything apart from the rational soul, I have no knowledge of it.

To return. Since I was lying dormant in the personal nature of the Father when he created creatures as a whole in his own nature, it follows that I was working with him. I was the work of God in which he made all things as giver, and I was then conscious in my personal nature of cooperating with the divine nature in this divine process. All the while I was working with him I was resting in God's nature exactly as I was in God before I was created. God made the universe and I with him, undefined but having substance in the Father.

Notice also, 'Through him all things were made' (John 1:3). If everything was made by him, and without him nothing was made, then I affirm that there is a power in the soul that is centred in the perennial now in the paternal heart and in the nature of God. Nor does it differ from the essential nature of God, except in being the created image of God. As one saint observes: 'What the soul cannot conceive by nature can never be hers by grace.' Like corn-seed dropped into the ground and lost to view, so the seed or spark in the soul is shed from the essential nature

of the Father, and is shining back into the incomprehensible essence, into that in which the soul conceives superin-
telligibly, blissfully. There, in beatific mode, stripped of
life and power, she returns to the uncreated good where,
robbed of every faculty, she is the image in the Trinity. As
our Lord said, 'That they may be one as we are one' (John
17:22). And when my soul, doffing her beatific habit, is
buried in the paternal field, in the living vine, as the Gospel says – when in this sense I lose myself and come into
my own as the rightful Son, then I make all things with
God, and the Word is in the beginning with God.

Take the next words, 'Without him nothing was made
that has been made' (John 1:3). I offer this interpretation.
In all rational creatures I find the quest for God. They
forge ahead according to the time and will bestowed on
them. But without him nothing is accomplished in those
creatures who, like the animals, stop at their outward
powers. Their mental works are worthless, lacking as they
do the divine light and spiritual freedom which gives them
permanence. Christ says, 'Every plant that my heavenly
Father has not planted will be pulled up by the roots'
(Matt. 15:13). That is all I want to say about this passage.

Take the next, ' . . . that has been made. In him was
life' (John 1:3–4). To see what this means, turn, O you
who are blessed, and commune with the understanding of
your uncreated intellect. ' . . . that has been made. In him
was the life.' In this eternal procession, in which all things
proceeded out from themselves, they were *now*, but in
time they were created from nothing and their life is in
him. As a result of this they are creatures, the effect of
that cause, the patent of his power resplendent in luminous detail. In this way we came out into time; but the revelation of himself to himself is in his eternal procession
where the knower is the same as the known, that is, in the
eternal emanation which is the Son from the Father, from
whom all things flow out. Thus what was made was the life
in him.

All rational creatures proceeded from God in the same way. Therefore I say that everything participates in every intellectual mode. I maintain that in her abstract understanding every rational soul knows the uncreated image which is her life. Now if my life and the life of all creatures is in God, I ask, 'Can God know himself in me without my soul?'

I answer: No. Man knows heat apart from the fire and light apart from the sun, but God cannot know himself without the soul. And why not? Because the soul is the out-flowing stream of the eternal deity and she is sealed in the image of the blessed Trinity. By this she knows she is God's creation. There I know the love of the divine fire by which rational creatures are illumined. I say: As the Father made me naked and free that I might stay and make my home in the groundless ground of the innermost heart of the Godhead, even so my soul must be utterly stripped if I am to be made supremely happy with God. As St Paul observes, 'He who unites himself with the Lord is one with him in spirit' (1 Cor. 6:17). The Father cannot know himself without me, since I stand in the ground of his eternal deity where his whole incomprehensible work is accomplished with me, and I am what is comprehended. By this I mean the light of the divine Sun, the universal life-giver. Therefore I see that God cannot know himself without me. 'That life was the light of men' (John 1:4).

Now understand the marvellous significance of this. What I am saying is that the life which is the light of men is man himself, understanding and conceiving himself in the wonder of the primordial power of the Father, in the leaping forth of his mysterious naught, in the blinding light of his indwelling Word brought out in eternal creation, albeit the uncreated nature of the nameless essence. It is his nature and his way, with perfectly receptive understanding, to take the incomprehensible essence for his own nature. By this the wonders of the negating nothing are revealed to him, the night of the mind becoming bright like noon in the light of his pure, primitive perfection, and his distinct, unutterable perfections shining out as clear as day. As David says, 'The night will shine like day, for darkness is as light to you' (Ps. 139:12).

And as his light is, so is his enlightenment, for in the naked essence man knows himself even as he is known. Knowing this, our Lord said, 'I am the gate for the sheep' (John 10:7). In these words he invites us to enter by the door of his flowing out and return into the source from which we came out, for this promises us something more than is offered us by the soul's beatitude.

Maybe you will say, 'Good brother, if the life has become the light of men, enabling them to know themselves as they are known, is it then possible for me to know myself as the very Son of God?'

I answer that the Son of God, our Lord Jesus Christ, is so attached to the Father's nature that never for an instant does he quit the paternal mode of deity. He accomplished his whole work in that nature and into that nature which gives being to all things, and he did so freely, in absolute idleness, for no reason at all. Here, bound to human nature, I have to work above nature freely, in absolute idleness or motionless quiet, in order not to be hindered by myself and by my personal nature and by things which are conditioned by time and are temporal. For to know all things in the cause of their existence, I must soar beyond all lights, temporal and eternal, and plunge into the causeless essence which gives mind and being to my soul. Drowned in this being, aware of self and things merely as being, my soul has lost her name. There remains there no nature but that which, in the Father, is eternally working with the Son, and as such I am a new man born in his nature and doing all I do supernaturally in the divine nature.

As our Lord said, 'I, when I am lifted up from the earth, will draw all men to myself' (John 12:32). So, being lifted up with all my powers into the uncreated good, I am one

body with Christ and one spirit with God, and I draw all
things to myself in one pure, perfect nature. As the Gospel says, 'This is my Son, whom I love; with him I am well
pleased' (Matt. 3:17). Knowing myself to be none other
than the Son of God, in that same sonship I am cast into
my middle power in the perennial now. Thus the eternal
Word is born in me unceasingly, as our Lord says,
'Father . . . Glorify your Son' (John 17:1). In this
interpretation lies the explanation of the words, 'It is
hard for a rich man to enter the kingdom of heaven'
(Matt. 19:23). Christ says in effect that the life is none
other than the naked spark alight within the soul, which
in the groundless Godhead knows itself to be none but
God, that is, the light which in rational creatures is splen-
did with the truth. I could give another meaning, but I
am afraid you would not follow it.

To continue: 'The light shines in the darkness, but the
darkness has not understood it' (John 1:5). I make no
comment here except to lament to the eternal truth that so
many fail to realise the high perfection, the deep happiness, glowing unseen within the soul. Christ says, 'Blessed
are the eyes that see what you see' (Luke 10:23). He did
not mean our bodily eyes, he meant those eyes that are
twin powers of the soul, set in her mind. As the Gospel
says, 'There came a man who was sent from God; his
name was John' (John 1:6). Truly, whether they are male
or female, these souls are John, for the word 'John'
denotes the grace of God.

What is grace? There is a faculty in the soul which is idle
and does no work; this is none other than the image of
God. Grace is not itself this image, but is its form which
reforms and transfigures the soul. In this re-formation in
which she has no form, in this transformation in which she
has all forms, the form that is every form, the soul is quiet.
She is self-contained because the truth is in her: not as
hers nor as a quality. As Christ said, 'I give them eternal
life' (John 10:28). Such a man is sent from God but is not

God-forsaken. Christ says, 'He who sent me does not send me alone, he also sends every one who does the will of my Father.'

There are four signs to tell a man that he is sent from God. First, that in time he is superior to time and temporal events. Second, being in time, he is detached from creatures. The third is that he is idle or quiet-minded. The fourth is that his nature does not keep changing. Christ said, 'I am that I am.' Possessing these signs, a man may take it that he is sent from God and his name is John for he is the grace of God itself. Hence Paul's words, 'God is my soul's new form wherein she is formless.'

Let us pass on: 'He came as a witness to testify concerning that light, so that through him all men might believe' (John 1:7). Examine this carefully. The words are open to a purely figurative interpretation. Just as John bore witness to the light of the divine unity concealed in Christ, in order that all might believe in him, so intuition, running ahead, gives the soul insight into the innermost recesses of the mind where there shines the spark which knows itself to be none other than the uncreated good of the ineffable deity. Then with all her powers the soul acknowledges and affirms the Son eternally in the Father and eternally born of the Father who is without beginning. As Christ said, 'Whoever hears my word and believes him who sent me has eternal life' (John 5:24).

Now take this in another sense. I will put a question and answer it myself: What reference has this to the true light?

Think, there is a power in the soul called mind which God sent with the soul. It is her storehouse of incorporeal forms and intellectual notions. The Father fashions this capacity of the soul in his outflowing divinity. By this means all the words of his divine essence flow distinctly into the word in our mind, just as memory pours out its treasure of images into the powers of the soul. When the soul sees the form of a rational creature, an angel's or her own form, the idea of the Father is clearly impressed in the soul angelically. But on penetrating deeper, into the very centre of the soul, the intellect finds God there face to face. And here, if she draws herself together to contemplate the vision of God in her, another of the soul's powers, called understanding, awakens, and the eternal Word is born, conceived by the soul while existing eternally in the Father. These two powers form one friendly disposition which gives direction to the intellect and is its will towards its source. When the spirit is flowing from the Father and the Son into this power and into all the powers she has, the soul, orientated to God, grows in knowledge of his image as her eternal prototype in God. She sees, too, how the holy Trinity is sealed in her. Thus the energies of the soul all bear witness to the light of the blessed Trinity that gives light to all mankind. They acknowledge and affirm and believe in the Son born in this man without ceasing. As the Gospel says, 'He himself was not the light; he came only as a witness to the light' (John 1:8).

Notice what follows: 'The true light that gives light to every man was coming into the world.' Open wide the ears of your understanding to catch the hidden meaning of the boundary between created and uncreated light which is plainly indicated in St John's words, 'That was the true light.' Taking the name 'John' to mean the light of grace, as I said above, I propose to show what may be rightly termed 'the true light that lights every man', which we receive direct.

I distinguish five lights. The first is devilish light; the second, natural light; the third, angelic light; the fourth, spiritual light; the fifth, divine light. Notice carefully how these five lights differ.

The first, or devilish light, leads everyone astray from the truth. This can be seen in cases where the outward self is not entirely in sympathy with the inward self. Suppose then that the inward self is sunk into his inner mind, where the eternal Word is born in the perennial now. The sudden shock of seeing the outward self pictured in the uncertain,

fluctuating light of time, will distort the light of his understanding and stop the eternal birth from taking place. This
shows it to be a devilish light, and you must therefore turn
away from it to the peace and quiet of your higher mind.
By this means, when Mary in her virginity was enlightened
by the Holy Spirit, she contrived to shun ideas of temporal
things and thus, transcending time, to harmonise her inner
and her outer selves into one settled calm, quite free from
images. This shows you the difference between this
devilish light and the divine light.

The second light is natural light. The line of demarca-
tion between natural light and the divine light comes
where the soul sees spirit directly, in very truth. When it
thinks by natural light, in random images, human nature is
changing, waxing and waning, aware of well-being and
distress, as Christ shows by his death and passion. But
when human nature is face to face with her true self she is
reflected into the divine nature. I ask, then, does the soul
in this natural light remain changeless in time? My answer
is no. That comes about when the soul is above time, in
union with the divine light and by the grace of God.
Drawn or caught up into the sweetness of the indwelling
spirit of God, the soul loves universal human nature as her
own nature, as God has been loving it eternally, in the
place where this nature is set over time in the light of
glory. Apart from this light, this man has the natural light
of indwelling grace, and at the point where he expresses
the idea, everything in this light of nature must fade away
out of time, as I have said. Mary was changeless by nature
as much as she was free from sinful occurrences in the idea
of her created nature in which she knew and loved all
mankind. Here you have the difference between the light
of nature in time and the light of that nature beyond time
in eternal glory. To me, it proves that all creatures are one
person, loving God by nature.

The third light is angelic light. Now you must know that
every individual angel is always open to any ideas that he

may choose, one more than another according to the individual character of his angelic nature. Their stability is not thereby impaired, provided they know and will and love in idleness. Lucifer had this uncreated understanding, and if in his creaturehood he had seen into the light of nature, and his creaturely nature had veered round in his angelic nature to his formless divine nature, he would never have fallen from the truth. As Isaiah observes, 'The angelic light in man is the means.' In the divine light the soul is not subject to ideas, nor can any shape appear to her, now that she knows, with a knowledge that transcends the soul's, of the incarnation of the Word. Even so, Mary, aloof in absolute purity of mind and body, knew creatures as a whole in super-angelic light. Her mind conceived no form except the unformed form of God, and she knew herself to be the ornament of God, not fashioned in the form of any creature. Therefore she cried, 'My spirit rejoices in God my Saviour' (Luke 1:47).

The fourth light is spiritual light, which is, moreover, the medium of the light of grace in the mind. In this light of the spirit you know how to order things in your mind with a view to the contemplation and enjoyment of the groundless essence in your soul.

· Absorbed in this, you are aware that the divine deep transcends the highest height of creatures. Why, I ask, was Peter oblivious of himself upon the mountain when Christ was transfigured before his three disciples? My answer is that the spiritual light of Peter's mind was eclipsed by the interior vision of the divine light: he forgot his own form on perceiving himself in this glory as the reflection ever streaming back to its paternal source. By formlessly apprehending in itself the bound Word to which Christ knew himself united, Peter was taking the Christ-image for his own image. However, he was not carried away into the divine light of the perfect intellect, but he was caught up into the spiritual light of its reflection as it shone back into its actual self. Mary was carried up beyond this spiritual light at the annunciation when she conceived the

Word in the word born according to the love of men.

The fifth light is divine light. There Mary always stood, carrying her gracious child. But Christ was born of her bodily. This birth transcends all sense and reason, and whoever is transported into this unveiled light perceives himself none other than that essence in which God has his being, his very Godhead. If with Mary we would carry this eternal Word, we must be caught up past the four lights into this fifth where we are ever giving birth to God in spirit as Mary carried him in the flesh.

To continue: 'He was in the world, and . . . the world did not recognise him' (John 1:10). Look at what was said above about the difference between created and uncreated light. These words refer to the world of his providential knowledge. When the world was in the Father as uncreated essence, his light, that is, his flowing intellect, was shining on this world-stuff in which the world existed in the Father in uncreated formless simplicity. But in its first eruption the world leapt out in many forms, though this multiplicity is essentially one. In this eruption this world was self-luminous light.

Notice a second interpretation of the words, 'He was in the world and the world was made by him.' By this world I understand none other than the divine man. See how this divine light may be called the world. Within his soul man has the power of being all creatures – stones, trees and all the rest of them – and in this same potentiality his mind has the universal prototype of individual creatures. So within the ambit of her five senses the soul is like rational and irrational creatures. In this sense the soul has both the form and matter, the rational and irrational natures of creatures in general.

In this sense all things were made in man. And by the same token, before God made everything, then hell, purgatory, everything, was God. Man is the world this light was in, this is the world that was made by him. John says, 'Through him all things were made; without him nothing was made that has been made.' From this I can only gather that multitudinous man is the world, that is, the world of darkness which did not understand the light referred to in Christ's words, 'I am the light of the world. Whoever follows me will never walk in darkness' (John 8:12). Here our Lord is inviting rational men to follow his example.

John goes on to say, 'He came to that which was his own, but his own did not receive him' (John 1:11). This refers to Christ, and I apply it to the individual soul as well. He is come into his own, and his own have neither known him nor accepted him. I say that whatever is found in Christ's nature is found in the highest power of the soul. Therefore God is man's own, but his own is not received by him. This refers to the intellectual five senses.

Clearly we have a parable of this in the woman at the well to whom Christ said, 'Call your husband.' The woman answered, 'I have no husband.' Christ said, 'You are right when you say you have no husband. The fact is, you have had five husbands, and the man you now have is not your husband' (John 4:16–18). I take it that her interest had been in her five senses. I interpret Christ's words, 'the man you now have is not your husband', to mean that she was neglecting the intellect she had, so it was no true man to her.

When God comes perceptibly to the soul, which is his own, he is received by what is not his own, that is, the outward senses and inward powers of the soul. When God is conceived imperceptibly by the soul, then we can say, 'Our home is in heaven.' This passage is clear in the light of these comments.

I, Brother John, put forward two questions. They concern the statement, 'Yet to all who received him, to those who believed in his name, he gave the right to become children of God' (John 1:12). In the first place, I ask, does the power to become God's sons lie with us or with God? In the second, I ask, what name do we believe in? My answers are briefly as follows.

To start with, it must be borne in mind that God is without will, without love, without justice, without mercy, indeed, without divinity or anything we can ascribe to him or predicate of him or attribute to him. For any good attributed to God or predicated of him simply reduces God to nothing. So the power, the ability to make this her own will lies with the soul. In her real will she is incapable of stooping to anything opposed to the nature of that will, and at the point where God and spirit vanish, in that same point I am the Son of God, born of God eternally, according to Christ's words, 'I am the only-begotten Son of God', for I am free from self in all creaturehood. Where I am, God is, and where God is, I am. Our joint love is God, and the one who dwells in this love dwells in God and God in him. Then the highest angel in heaven is mine, as much as he is God's. By God's power and by God's might we make ourselves God's sons, for he empowers us with himself, penetrating the will of the soul even as Father and Son permeate their common Spirit. That is the answer to the first question, to the best of my knowledge at present.

Now to answer the second question: What divine name do we believe in? That is written in the Gospel in Christ's words, 'Now this is eternal life: that they may know you, the only true God' (John 17:3). Truth is God, and love, as truly as God is God. If God is free from names, then I dare not think that I have the name of Henry or Conrad or Ulric, for by adding anything to God I block him with an idol. But anyone who believes in the name of God rejoices in the universal name, that is, the divine name which we believe in. In this unfathomable light of faith, faith makes us of multitudinous knowledge ignorant, of multitudinous will without volition, in multitudinous form unshapen. And so the prophet says, 'I said, "You are 'gods'"' (Ps. 82:6). Believing in the name of God, we are God's sons. If anyone is able to give a better answer to these two questions, I would like to hear it.

John goes on to say, 'Children born not of natural descent, nor of human decision or a husband's will' (John

1:13). Flesh and blood and unconquered human will cannot possess the kingdom of heaven till they are born again
in God. This is quite clear, the meaning is obvious to all.
But I desire to speak briefly on the subject of manhood.

The highest power of the soul is the man, that is, the
soul's will, which always stands bare and uncovered. The
second is intellect, the woman, who is always veiled, and
the lower is raised up to the higher. Now when the power
we call the man, that is, the will, is joined to the power we
call the woman, that is to say, the intellect, then the
woman brings forth fruit in the perennial now. When the
male is parted from the female, man's will is wavering in
false light. The apostle truly says, 'The Word became
flesh' (John 1:14).

The manhood of Christ as seeing into God has a reflection in the Father's personal nature. In the groundless substance of the Godhead human nature stands perfectly
steady, gazing down in the transcendent light for love of
creatures. Thus divine and human nature are at one in
human nature. And by the same token, even if Adam had
not fallen, Christ would still have been made man because
of the love proceeding from God. This love is always being
born in eternity in the divine nature and was bound to
become man in Christ because of the character of that
nature which flowed for ever out of the groundless ground
of God. The smallest spark falling out of the least and lowest of the angels would illuminate and outshine this world
and it would dim the brightest lights of human and angelic
nature if it shone next to God. So Christ restores human
nature, not angelic nature. As his divinity lay hidden in his
humanity when 'the Word became flesh' in him, so let us
hide our human nature in his divine nature in that same
Word which was incarnate. By living the Christ-life more
than my own life, I am Christ rather than myself and my
proper name is Christ rather than James or John. And so
it happens that beyond time I am changed into God.

Now listen to another meaning: the incarnation of the

Word in the sacrament. He made his body in the sacrament by word and knowledge and gave it to his disciples idly, that is to say, without motion or passion, and this sacrament was not consummated by knowledge alone but by words as well. In the same way I observe that in the highest power of the soul, which corresponds to the Father-nature, intellect gave birth to itself in the image of Divinity to strike into this Word as perfect will. And in the groundless love of this same will the Holy Spirit was begotten in the Word with this same intellect. And this birth still continues in the sacrament for those who are rightly called Christ. These people are true priests and live in the truth, for their going is above the angels and they are not to be touched by temporal things. As Christ said to Mary Magdalene, 'Do not hold on to me, for I have not yet returned to the Father' (John 20:17), so these souls are truly risen with Christ. God gives himself freely, idly, as he gave himself to his disciples in token of the love which works the same in us, and those who take this sacrament as freely and resignedly and unhindered by the self, receive it as truly as the giver gives it. And anyone who takes it in any other way does not wholly and solely give himself to the truth. When in the sacrament I receive God from God supersacramentally in this way, I am actually changed into what I receive. Thus the Word is made flesh and dwells among us mystically. Wherever this is realised there is the proof of the divine spark. Moreover, I am bold enough to say that if anyone were prepared to receive outward food as he receives the sacrament, he would receive God as much as he does in the sacrament. Many people find this hard to accept, though it is quite consistent with the truth, for the gift prepares us for its reception, and I should be the thing prepared for that which has prepared me. St John says, 'We have seen his glory, the glory of the One and Only, who came from the Father, full of grace and truth' (John 1:14). I gather from this that anyone who knows the joys of the divine life shines within and without like the only Son of God. As St Paul says, 'I no longer live, but Christ lives in me' (Gal. 2:20).

Consider what is meant by sons of God and children of
God. To be God's children in the sense that he created us
is not enough. For instance, if I paint my likeness on the
wall, anyone seeing the likeness is not seeing me; but anyone who sees me sees my likeness, and not merely my likeness, but my child. If I really knew my soul, anyone who
saw my conception of it would say it was my son, for I
share my energy and nature with it. As it is here, so it is in
the Godhead. The Father understands himself perfectly
clearly, so his image, that is, his Son, appears to him. The
Father is light, the Son is light and image, and the Holy
Spirit is also light and image. Inasmuch as the Father
imagines or conceives his Son, he is called Son, and inasmuch as he endows him with his nature, he is called his
child. In the same way a man is the image of God if, being
detached from things, he is living as spirit in the spirit of
God. Such people have glory and honour as the only Son
of God, full of the grace and truth of the reflection of
God. They really contain and possess God in themselves;
thus the kingdom of God is within us.

This ends the commentary on John's Gospel.

PART III

SAYINGS

SAYINGS

1

Meister Eckhart said in a sermon that the work wrought by God in the God-loving soul which he finds empty and detached enough for him to bring himself to spiritual birth in her, this work gives God greater pleasure than any work he ever did with any creature. It is far nobler than the creation of all things from nothing.

On being asked the reason why this work gives God such pleasure, he said it is because out of all God's creatures, only the soul has a capacity large enough for him to empty his entire might, the whole ground of his being, into it. This he does in the act of giving birth to himself spiritually in the soul.

When asked what God's birth is, he said that God's being born within the soul is nothing other than God's self-revelation to the soul in some new knowledge and in some new mode.

Then they asked him, 'Does the soul's chief happiness consist in this act by which God gives birth to himself in her in a spiritual way?'

He said, 'Though it is true that God takes greater pleasure in this act than in any other deed he ever did in relation to creatures, nevertheless, the soul is happier being re-born into God. God's birth in her does not make her completely happy: she is supremely happy when, in love and praise, she follows the wisdom in which she is born back to its source and, in their common origin, holding to what is his, she lets go of what is her own. So she is happy not in hers, but his.

2

Meister Eckhart said: A man of godly love and godly fear and perfect faith may, if he will, receive God's body every day at the priest's hands.

3

The question is: What does God do in heaven? The answer given by the saint is this: He crowns his own work. The works for which God crowns his saints he worked in them himself.

Meister Eckhart says: I have been asked what God is doing in heaven. My answer is that he has been giving birth to his Son eternally, he is giving birth now and will go on giving birth to him for ever, for the Father is in childbirth in every virtuous soul. Happy, three times happy, is the man within whose soul the heavenly Father is thus brought to bed. All she surrenders to him here she will enjoy from him in life eternal. God made the soul on purpose for her to bear his own Son. His son's spiritual birth in Mary was more pleasing to God than his nativity in the flesh. When this birth happens nowadays in the good, loving soul, it gives God greater pleasure than his creation of the heavens and earth.

4

Meister Eckhart says: The man who is at home everywhere is Godworthy. God is present to the man who is always the same. God gives birth to his own Son in the man in whom creatures are stilled.

5

Meister Eckhart says: Holy Scripture cries aloud for freedom from self. To be self-free is to be self-controlled, and to be self-controlled is to be self-possessed, and self-possession is God-possession and possession of everything God ever made. I tell you, as truly as God is God and I am a man, if you were quite free from self, free from the highest angel, then the highest angel would be yours as well as your own self. This method gives self-mastery.

6

According to Meister Eckhart, grace only comes with the Holy Spirit. It bears the Holy Spirit upon its back. Grace is no stationary thing. It is ever-becoming. It flows straight out of God's heart. Grace does nothing but re-form and convey into God. Grace makes the soul godlike. God, the ground of the soul and grace go together.

7

Meister Eckhart says: The man to whom God is different in one thing from another, and to whom God is dearer in one thing than another, that man is a barbarian, still in the wilds, a child. The man to whom God is the same in everything has come to adulthood. But the man to whom creatures all mean a sense of want and exile has come into his own.

He was also asked: 'Does the man who goes out of himself need to trouble at all about his nature?'

He answered: 'God's yoke is easy and his burden is light. No, he only needs to trouble about his will. What the beginner fears is the expert's delight. The kingdom of God is for none but the thoroughly dead.'

8

Meister Eckhart said: In the cause of charity, someone who lends himself to receiving a hand-out of bread is better than someone who gives a hundred marks. How do I make that out? I argue in this way. Doctors of theology agree that honour is of far more worth than temporal goods. Now the man who gives a hundred marks for charity gets back in praise and honour more than his hundred marks' worth. The hand he stretches out with gifts collects both more and better than it gave. But the beggar reaching out his hand for bread is exchanging it for his honour. The giver buys honour but the taker sells it.

Another thing gives the beggar who receives the advantage over the giver who gave the hundred marks to God. The giver glories in and gratifies his nature, the beggar is subduing his and flouting his nature. The giver is made much of for his gifts, the beggar is scorned and shunned for taking them.

9

Meister Eckhart said: I never ask God to give himself to me, I beg him to purify, to empty, me. If I am empty, God of his very nature is obliged to give himself to me to fill me.

How to be pure? By steadfast longing for the one good, that is, God.

How to acquire this longing? By self-denial and dislike of creatures. Self-knowledge is the way, for creatures are all nothing, they come to nothing with grief and bitterness.

Since God is pure good in himself, he can dwell nowhere except in the pure soul. He overflows into her, he flows wholly into her.

What does emptiness mean? It means a turning from creatures, the heart lifted up to the perfect good so that creatures are no comfort nor is there any need for them except when the perfect good, that is God, may be grasped in them. The clear eye tolerates the speck no more than the pure soul tolerates anything that clouds, that comes between her and God. When she enjoys creatures they are all pure for she enjoys them in God and God in creatures. She is so limpid that she sees through herself. Nor is God far to seek: she finds him in herself when in her natural purity she flows into the supernatural pure Godhead where she is in God and God in her. And what she does she does in God and God does it in her.

10

Meister Eckhart said: To die the death in love and knowledge is more noble and of greater worth than all the good works that Christendom has done in love and knowledge from its beginning until now and will do till the judgment day. These only serve to bring this death about, this death in which life eternal springs.

11

Meister Eckhart says: We fail to get our way with God because we lack two things: profound humility and an effective will. Upon my life I swear that God in his divinity is capable of all things, but this he cannot do – when the soul has these two things, he cannot leave her unsatisfied. Therefore do not fret about trivialities; you were not made for trivial things, and the glory of the world is only a travesty of truth, only a heresy of happiness.

12

When Meister Eckhart was asked about God's greatest gift to him, he answered: There are three. First, cessation of carnal desires and pleasures. Secondly, divine light which enlightens me in everything I do. Thirdly, daily I grow and am renewed in virtue, grace and happiness.

13

On one occasion Brother Eckhart said: There are five things which are sure signs in whoever has them that he will never lapse from God. First, though this man experiences terrible things from God or man, he never complains: no word but praise and thanks is ever heard.

Again, at the most trying times he never says one word in his defence.

Thirdly, this man desires from God what God will freely give, and nothing else: he leaves it all to God.

Fourthly, nothing in heaven or earth can ruffle him. So settled is his calm that heaven and earth in topsyturvydom would leave him quite content in God.

Fifth, nothing in heaven or earth can cheer him; for having reached the point where nothing in heaven or earth can sadden him, so neither can it gladden him, except as trifles can.

A man as remote and as far from his own self as is the

chief angel of the Seraphim will possess that angel for his own if he is God's and God is his. And that is the bare truth, as God is God.

St Paul says: 'May I never boast except in the cross of our Lord Jesus Christ, through which the world has been crucified to me, and I to the world' (Gal. 6:14).

14

Meister Eckhart, the preacher, said: There is no greater valour and no sterner fight than that for self-effacement, self-oblivion.

15

Brother Eckhart said: Not all suffering is rewarded, but only the suffering that is cheerfully consented to. A man hanged on the gallows, suffering unwillingly, would prefer it to have been someone else. There is no reward for that. It is the same with other sufferings. It is not the suffering that counts, it is the virtue. To anyone who does not suffer out of love, I say that to suffer is suffering, and it is hard to bear. But anyone who suffers for love does not suffer and his suffering is fruitful in God's sight.

16

Anyone who would be what he ought to be must stop being what he is. When God made the angels, the first sight they saw was that of the Father with the Son sprouting out of his Father's heart like a green shoot out of a tree. They have had this blissful vision for more than six thousand years, and how it comes about they know as well today as when they were first made. This is because of their keen perception: the more we know, the less we understand.

17

'And so shall a man order his life if he would be perfect.' Concerning this, Meister Eckhart says: Works wrought from within are pleasant both to God and man; they are kindly, living works. They are Godworthy, for it is God alone who accomplishes in man works wrought from within – the prophet Isaiah says, 'Lord . . . all that we have accomplished you have done for us' (Isa. 26:12). Christ, too, said, 'The miracles I do in my Father's name . . . ' (John 10:25). Man finds such works both easy and pleasant, for all deeds are agreeable and pleasant when body and soul are harmonious. This is the case in all these works.

Again, these works are living works. A dead animal differs from a living animal in that the dead creature is moved from outside only, that is, it must be pulled or pushed, and its works are all dead works. The live animal moves itself wherever it wants, its motivational power is within and its works are living works. In the same way, those works of men which have their source within, from the centre of our being, where God moves by himself, these are our works, divine works, useful works. But works which come from some external cause and not from our inner being, these works, I say, are dead. They are not godly works nor are they ours.

Meister Eckhart also says: Works wrought from within are willing works. But that which is willing is sweet. Therefore works from within are all pleasant, whereas works due to any outward cause are unwilling and slavish, for if nothing were moving from the outside, no work would be done at all. So this work is reluctant, menial, bitter.

18

Meister Eckhart said: In this life no person can reach the point where he is excused from outward works. Even if someone follows the contemplative life, he cannot altogether keep from flowing out and mingling in the life of action. Even as a penniless man may still be generous in the will to give, and a man of means who gives nothing cannot be called generous, so no one can have virtues without exercising virtue at the proper time and place. Hence those who lead the contemplative life and do no outward works are quite mistaken and entirely on the wrong tack. What I say is that someone who lives the contemplative life may, indeed, must, be absolutely free from outward works when engaged in the act of contemplation, but afterwards his duty lies in doing outward works. For no one can live the contemplative life without a break, and an active life bridges the gaps in the life of contemplation.

19

Why is it, Meister Eckhart asks, that people are so slow to look for God in earnest? His comment is: When one is looking for a thing and finds no trace of its existence, one hunts half-heartedly and in distress. But if one comes across some trace of the quarry, the chase grows lively, light-hearted and keen. The man in quest of fire is cheered when he feels the heat and looks for its source with eagerness and pleasure. And so it is with those in quest of God: feeling none of the sweetness of God, they grow listless, but sensing the sweetness of divinity, they cheerfully pursue their search for God.

20

Meister Eckhart asks: Whose are the prayers God always hears? And he answers: Whoever worships God as God, God hears. But the man who worships God for worldly goods, worships not God: he worships what he worships God for, and employs God as his servant to help him get it. As St Augustine puts it: 'What you love you worship; true prayer, real prayer, is nothing but loving: what you love, that you pray to.' Hence, no one prays to God aright except the one who prays to God for God without a thought of anything but God.

21

According to Meister Eckhart, God is not only the Father of all good things, but he is the mother of all things as well. He is Father, for he is the cause of all things and their creator. He is the mother, for when creatures have received their being from him he still stays with them to keep them in being. If God did not remain with his creatures after they had started their own life, they would quickly fall out of being. Falling from God means falling from being into nothingness. It is not so with other causes, they can safely leave the things they cause when these have gained their own being. When the house is in being its builder can depart. The reason is that the house is not made by the builder alone: the builder takes his building materials from nature. But God provides the creature with the whole of what it is, with form as well as matter, so he is bound to stay with it or it will promptly drop out of existence.

22

Meister Eckhart also said: My lowliness raises up God, and the lower I humble myself the higher I exalt God, and the higher I exalt God the more gently and sweetly he pours into me his divine gift, his divine inflowing. For the higher the inflowing thing, the easier and smoother its flow.

How God is raised upon my lowliness I explain like this: the lower I abase myself and the more I keep myself down, the higher God towers above me. The deeper the trough, the higher the crest. In just the same way, the more I abase and humble myself, the higher God goes and the better and more easily he pours his divine influx into me. So it is true that I exalt God by my lowliness.

23

Whosoever has three things is beloved of God. The first is removal of goods, the second is removal of friends, and the third is removal of self.

24

According to Meister Eckhart, there are seven degrees of contemplation. Let whoever wishes to practise contemplation seek out a quiet spot and set himself to thinking, first, how noble his soul is, how she has flowed straight out of God, a thought that fills him with a great delight.

Having seriously considered this, let him next think how much God must love his soul to make it in the likeness of the Trinity, so that all God is by nature he may be by grace. He will inevitably take even greater delight in this, for it is far more noble to be made in the form of the Trinity than merely to come straight from God.

In the third stage he meditates on the fact that he has been loved by God for ever. The Trinity has been for ever and God has loved the soul for ever.

Fourthly, he reflects that God has always instructed him to enjoy with God what God has always enjoyed and always will, that is, God himself.

At the fifth stage, the soul enters into herself and knows God in herself. This happens in this way: no being can be without being, and being feeds on being; but being cannot live upon this food till the food is converted to the same blessed nature as that which feeds upon it, and this applies to being which is being-of-itself. But there is no being-of-itself except God. So my soul is living on nothing but God. And by entering into oneself like this one finds God in oneself. If it is God's will that I do not faint, he must give me being. No being can stand without God, so if he means me to have being then he must give me himself.

The sixth stage is when the soul knows herself in God. It happens in this way: everything in God is God. Now my idea has always been in God, it is now, and always will be. Therefore my soul is always one with God and is God, and I find myself in God in the exalted fashion of being God in God eternally. This brings the expert soul unutterable delight.

At the seventh stage the soul knows God in himself as being without beginning, and as the source of all things. This secret knowledge comes to no man fully in this life, for it means the beholding of God, a thing not of this world.

25

God will never give himself to the soul . . . unless she brings her husband, that is, her whole free will.

26

What the joy of the Lord is no one can tell. But note this much concerning it. The joy of the Lord is the Lord himself, no one else, the Lord being living, essential, actual intellect which knows itself and is and lives itself in itself and is the same. I do not saddle it with any mode, indeed, I divest it of all modes, for he himself is modeless mode who is and is glad because he is. This is the joy of the Lord and is the Lord himself. White is not black, nor is aught naught. From naught naught can be taken. From aught aught can be taken, and it is wholly like that with God. Of aught that is wholly in God naught remains. The soul joined to God has in him, once and for all, all that is at all, in absolute perfection. There the soul forgets things and herself, as she is in herself, waking up in God, godlike as God in her, so much in love with her self in him, so indiscriminately one with him, that she enjoys naught but him, delighting in him. What more should she know or desire?

27

The first work of God in the soul is the birth of his Son in the soul, and from this act his other gifts – such as grace and virtue – flow into the soul. What God can do in the soul is to bring forth his Son in the soul, and this must happen. It is characteristic of God that he cannot refrain, he must give birth to his Son in me and in you all. I say that God gives birth to me, his Son, and so, I say, to you all as well. That we are all born the Son of God is nothing wonderful; we can see this with creatures. Now note my words: this man is the *not*. I am not what you are, and you are not what I am. Suppress the *not* and we are just the same; take naught from creatures and creatures are all the same. The remainder is one. What is this one? It is the Son the Father bears. To be the actual Son the Father bears we must cancel the naught

of creatures. This naught which all creatures are encumbers
a man and stops him being the very Son born of the Father.
God tells us to part with naught in order to be the selfsame
Son the Father bears. For this man must be one. He must
escape from images and forms before he can be the actual
Son the Father brings to birth. He must be rid of everything, not merely alien things, but even his own. For God's
Son and man's son are not two sons, they are one Son, one
nature. So a man must run from other natures as well as
from his own and stand in the bare nature of the Son in the
Godhead, in that only. If one is to be the actual Son the
Father bears, one must give up one's own nature
altogether.

'But many people have natures so alien to their own, how
then can they surrender their own nature?'

We must always surrender our own natures in order to
become the very Son the Father bears. As St Paul says, 'For
those God foreknew he also predestined to be conformed
to the likeness of his Son' (Rom. 8:29). In other words,
since the Son alone is beloved of the Father, whatever
things the Father loves he must love them in his Son, and as
we become this Son the Father bears, we are changed into
his Son of love and are his very Son. You can be sure of this:
God will love them in us and in all creatures in the guise of
his only-begotten Son, providing we abandon naught and
become estranged from naught. We must relinquish all
things, must forget all things, keeping nothing but the
single nature of the Son. It seems a great deal, but it is not.
It is a simple thing that God bids us do, he bids us give up
naught. Whoever is without cause has given up naught, and
by doing this we gain the whole world in abundance. All
things come to the good man – be sure of that. If I am better
than you are, all the good you do and what you have are
mine rather than yours, for what you have you have in
naught. But if I have abandoned naught, I am the very Son
the Father bears, and everything belongs to me in God.

28

What could be sweeter than to have a friend with whom, as with yourself, you can discuss all that is in your heart?

29

When God made man, the innermost heart of the Godhead was put into man.